Everyday
Delicious

Everyday Delicious

30 MINUTE(ISH) HOME-COOKED MEALS MADE SIMPLE

Rocco DiSpirito

PHOTOGRAPHS BY JONATHAN PUSHNIK

RODALE
New York

Contents

Classic Pastas & Noodles

Sandwiches & Big Salads

Crudos, Simple Fish & Marinated Dishes

Savory Seafood

Perfect Poultry

Mouthwatering Meats

Sunday Suppers
Leisurely Recipes for Gatherings & Special Occasions

Introduction

*In its own way, food is the language we use to express
our life stories, through every phase, twist, and turn.*

The dishes we cook tell the story of where we come from, the people
we hold dear, and the moments of hardship or abundance. We tell
the stories of the winter when we didn't have enough time, and
the summer when we had too much time. We tell the stories of the
people we've lost and gained, the experiences that shaped us, the
year we saw the world, and the year we saw only our apartment.

This book is a record of my personal journey through food, and
my desire to share it with you so that you may enhance your own
story. I grew up in a big Italian family where meals were savored
over conversation. Food was prepared with love and with a larger
purpose in mind. Food fed more than our bodies; it fed our souls.
Meals were about connecting, sharing, and nourishing.

As time passed, life got in the way—as I'm sure it does for
most of us. My entire adult life has been spent either cooking
for others in professional kitchens or teaching home cooks how
to make healthy, nutritious meals without sacrificing flavor. It's
been incredibly rewarding professionally, but behind the scenes,
I almost never joined the table to appreciate the meal myself.
As my career progressed, the personal joy of home cooking and
the significance it held became distant. The light that came from
cooking for myself, family, and friends—a formative part of my
childhood—had dimmed.

Everything changed during the Covid-19 pandemic. I, like
most of us, found myself at home, cooking and sitting down for
meals surrounded by family. I was doing what I love, for the
people I love, for the first time in decades. I started preparing the
meals I relished making when no one was watching, the meals
that were meant to nourish and bring comfort when I wasn't
worried about counting every calorie. I once again felt the power
of cooking and enjoying weekday meals with my family—an
everyday luxury for some that for me had become a rarity at best.

Of course, I'm not immune to the labor of cooking: It can be hard work. As a home cook preparing nightly meals, I also experienced the fatigue of spending hours planning and cooking every night, and the frustration of making the same dish again and again. I found myself trying to remember those favorite simple go-to recipes from my youth, recipes that were passed down in my family for generations, the dishes I learned to make growing up in the vibrant city of New York, and the recipes I created and loved during my years in professional kitchens.

Day by day, I started writing down ideas. My notebook became filled with scribbles and inspirations and notes like "Mom's smashed garlic" or "Dad's fish market trips" or "Robert's mom's ceviche." I started cooking from the heart, from my memories and my stories.

That's what inspired this book. Incoherent scribbles in my notebook became a collection of over one hundred of the best no-fuss recipes that have stuck with me throughout the years.

These are my absolute top recipes from over forty years spent cooking.

The best part? These are also the dishes made by the hardworking moms I learned from growing up who didn't have all day to spend in the kitchen, and the busy restaurants I worked in where it needed to be ready 5 minutes ago. The vast majority of these recipes come together in 30 minutes or less, with flavors that will stick with you for the rest of your life.

If I've come to understand one thing, it's that food brings joy. I've watched food bring comfort and moments of hope, even during the dog days of the pandemic. We've returned to our busy work schedules, commutes, and obligations, but we find ourselves with a new understanding of what we can accomplish in our kitchen, and a renewed excitement to share in life around the table. What we've lost in the bargain, though, is time.

In this book, I'll teach you the tools, ingredients, and tricks I use to build flavor quickly, with foolproof recipes you can turn to time and time again. That means less planning, less prep, less time cooking, and more time enjoying meals with the ones you love.

These are the recipes I turn to when I have 30 minutes to spare and just a few ingredients in my pantry. They're the meals I make for myself at home, or to please a crowd, or just on a Sunday evening when my downstairs neighbor, chef buddy, and best friend's five-year-old are all breaking bread at my table.

Be it a weeknight Penne alla Vodka (page 27) with your family, Butterscotch-Glazed Short Ribs (page 247) for Sunday supper with your friends, or a Crab & Heirloom Tomato Salad (page 103) for a lazy summer afternoon on the porch, you're sure to find an exciting take on your favorite classic, or a recipe to start a brand-new tradition of your own.

With food's ability to tell our story, to connect and unite in even the most difficult times, I can't think of a better time than now to share these recipes with you. You'll be shocked by how quickly your own stories and traditions come together—and how much time you have to spare.

Buon appetito!

Rules to Cook By

Great cooking doesn't require hours and hours in the kitchen. You just need to know the tricks of the trade to save time without sacrificing flavor. Here are some of my rules to cook by to help you have success every night of the week.

Condiments Are King

A handy trick that hasn't caught on in the United States, but certainly should, is how store-bought condiments easily and instantly add depth to your home cooking.

Outside of mustard, mayo, and ketchup, all of which I love as much as the next person, there are complex, high-quality condiments from around the world available in your everyday grocery store. To get big flavor fast, I use condiments as a seasoning, like adding nuoc cham to enhance my Too-Easy Vietnamese Beef Salad (page 89) with bright, umami-rich punchiness, or using Bull-Dog tonkatsu sauce to add a sweet and deeply savory complexity to the gravy in Pork Chops in Bacon Gravy (page 227).

To achieve such nuanced flavor, I would need to spend hours stewing and reducing and seasoning and tasting and seasoning again, or months fermenting anchovies in my backyard, or whisking and preserving—you get the idea. Instead, I merely pop open a jar and grab a spoon.

The (Not-So-Basic) Pantry Basics to Stock Up On

HERE, in no particular order, are my go-to flavor boosters, from condiments to spice blends to pickles and more, that may not already be living in your pantry. While some of these items may be readily available at your local market, others may require a bit more searching. Have no fear, all can be easily sourced online.

Sambal oelek: Indonesian chili paste made from ground chiles, vinegar, and salt, sambal oelek adds a spicy and savory depth of flavor to a wide variety of dishes, from stir-fries and marinades to soups and sauces, or can be used as a condiment.

Furikake: Japanese seasoning blend made from dried fish, sesame seeds, and seaweed, furikake can be used during cooking or as a topping to impart a savory umami flavor.

Kewpie mayo: Like American mayonnaise, but creamier, sweeter, and slightly tangier, Kewpie mayo adds a nice richness and texture.

Sweet soy sauce: Also known as kecap manis, sweet soy sauce is thicker, sweeter, and less salty than regular soy sauce. I like to use it to add a subtle sweetness to savory dishes.

Dark soy sauce: Made by fermenting standard soy sauce for longer, dark soy sauce is thicker and less salty, and has deeper, more complex flavor. With its robust flavor, a little goes a long way to adding richness to dipping sauces, soups, marinades, and more.

Yuzu kosho: Japanese condiment made from yuzu (an East Asian citrus often described as a cross between a lemon and a mandarin orange), chile peppers, and salt. Sour, spicy, and salty, yuzu kosho adds a bright, spicy flavor to soups, marinades, dressings. A small spoonful is perfect on sashimi. The list goes on.

S&B prepared mustard: Like American mustard with a kick, Japanese S&B prepared mustard is a spicier and more complex version of what's probably in your refrigerator. I love it for cutting the richness of fatty meats.

Bull-Dog tonkatsu sauce: A sweet and savory Japanese sauce that's typically used as a dipping sauce for tonkatsu (deep-fried pork cutlet), Bull-Dog makes a welcome, umami-rich addition to marinades, or is delicious as a dipping sauce for fried foods.

Passata: A sieved tomato puree made from fresh ripe tomatoes, passata makes the perfect base for quick tomato sauces as its smooth, thick consistency means it doesn't require long simmering. It is often also labeled "tomato puree."

Tamarind puree/ concentrate: A thick, dark brown paste made from the pulp of the tamarind fruit, tamarind puree is commonly found in Southeast Asian, Indian, and Mexican cuisine and adds a sour and slightly sweet flavor to savory and sweet dishes and drinks.

Preserved radish: Also known as chai po, preserved radish is often used in Chinese cuisine to give a sweet, salty, and tangy flavor.

Harissa: A spicy chile, garlic, olive oil, and spice paste that originated in Tunisia, harissa is commonly used in North African and Middle Eastern cuisine to impart heat and smokiness, with a hint of sweetness and earthiness.

Ghee: A type of clarified butter frequently used in Indian cuisine, ghee is made by simmering butter to remove the milk solids and water. It has a rich, nutty flavor and a higher smoke point than regular butter, making it great for high-heat cooking methods.

Rose harissa powder: A blend of ground chiles, spices, and dried rose petals, rose harissa powder is a North African and Middle Eastern spice that adds a floral aroma and subtle sweetness.

Sichuan peppercorns: A key ingredient of Sichuan cuisine, the most prominent feature of Sichuan peppercorns is their numbing effect, along with their more subtle floral and citrus flavor notes.

Garlic puree: Sometimes labeled as "garlic paste." Keeping garlic puree on hand will save you a lot of time when you want a concentrated garlic flavor. In most cases, it's not a great substitute for minced garlic. I've called for garlic puree only when it works best.

Chicken demi-glace: An extra-rich, concentrated stock, demi-glace adds complex flavor and sometimes texture to a recipe. It can be homemade or purchased online or in specialty grocery stores.

Chili crisp: Try chili crisp once and you'll become a connoisseur, especially with the wide variety available to choose from. It tastes great on just about anything—from salads to eggs to soups and stews— you'll want to stock up because the jars don't last long.

Shaoxing wine: A type of Chinese rice wine that is commonly used in Eastern Chinese cuisine, Shaoxing wine gives a slightly sweet and nutty flavor, perfect for sauces, soups, marinades, and deglazing.

Oyster sauce: Made from oyster extract, sugar, and salt, oyster sauce has a deeply savory and slightly sweet flavor. It's delicious for adding depth to marinades, as a seasoning, or even as a dipping sauce.

Nuoc cham: A popular dipping sauce in Vietnamese cuisine, nuoc cham is made from fish sauce, lime juice, sugar, garlic, chiles, water, and vinegar. The perfect balance of sweet, sour, salty, and spicy, it's a versatile sauce that can be used as everything from a dip to a dressing to a marinade.

Gochujang: A traditional Korean fermented chile paste made from ground chiles, glutinous rice powder, meju (dried fermented soybean) powder, and salt, gochujang has a deep, savory, and spicy flavor with a hint of sweetness.

Parmigiano-Reggiano cheese: Of all pantry items, Parmigiano-Reggiano is the nearest and dearest to my heart. It's the number one ingredient I always keep stocked. Deeply savory and complex, there is no substitute for real Parmigiano-Reggiano (including pecorino!).

Use Your Resources

If chefs know how to do one thing well, it's how to use their resources: Don't feel like you have to make everything from scratch for a dish to be "home cooked." Instead, use all the tools and resources at your disposal. Throughout this book, I never give a "shortcut" I don't wholeheartedly stand behind. Whenever possible, I offer ways you can cut back on time without sacrificing quality.

Go ahead and let your butcher slice the rib eye for your Philly Cheesesteaks (page 73). Use rotisserie chicken for Chicken Tinga Enchiladas in Adobo Sauce (page 166) or store-bought poached shrimp for Shrimp Cocktail with Spicy Chili Mayo (page 100). Take-out fried rice saves you a step in my Fat-Fried Rice (page 152), and prune baby food replaces homemade prune puree in First-Draft Fried Pork Chops in Prune Butter Sauce (page 223). As someone who's dedicated countless hours of his life to being the best cook possible, I'd never sacrifice a necessary step just to save a few minutes. I do, however, give you plenty of the tips and tricks I've learned to save you time *and* yield exceptional results.

In this book, we work smarter, not harder, to create delicious, comforting home-cooked meals in a fraction of the time.

Mise It Out

One of the most significant differences between how home cooks and professional chefs work is the concept of *mise en place*, meaning "everything in its place." It's the idea that all your ingredients are measured, prepped, and ready to go before you turn on the stove.

The secret to success with many quick-cooking dishes is high heat, which demands your full attention. If you hear that voice in your head saying, "I can just chop the celery while the onions are browning," ignore it. I've written these recipes to be cooked very quickly—most in under 30 minutes—and having all your ingredients ready to go is an important first step to not only make this happen, but have fun doing it.

Having that celery washed, chopped, and ready to go will help you cook more efficiently and effectively. It allows you to focus on cooking, stay organized, and avoid any last-minute scrambling to find that crucial ingredient you need. It's also your chance to double-check that you have everything and avoid any last-minute trips to the store. Overall, taking the time to prepare your mise en place before cooking will make the cooking process smoother, more efficient, and less stressful.

Sometimes It's Worth It

I set out to create a cookbook of 30-minute meals that are luxurious enough for a party yet simple enough to make on a weeknight. Easy! That's how I like to cook.

Take the Lobster with Lemony Red Pepper Butter & Popovers (page 265), a perfectly festive New Year's Eve dinner that's ready in just 25 minutes, or a weeknight 1, 2, 3 Shabu-Shabu Hot Pot (page 208) with thinly shaved beef that comes together in just 15 minutes and change.

With that said, on special occasions, like someone's birthday, a big holiday, or just a lazy day in which you have the luxury of time, there is something incredibly nurturing about a slow-cooked meal, like Garlic & Horseradish Crusted Rib Roast with Root Vegetable & Red Wine Gravy (page 241). I didn't want to exclude my favorite recipes because they didn't fit into a strict rule or cookbook title, so I've included all of them in the Sunday Suppers chapter. After all, some of my favorite go-to dishes of all time take a little longer to prepare—and it would have been a shame to leave out these more splurge-worthy items.

My promise to you is this: Any dish that demands your patience will be worth the extra time. You can't get a buttery, juicy prime rib in under an hour, but for the person in your life who merits the extra work, it'll be worth every minute.

Classic Pastas & Noodles

Spaghetti Pomodoro 365

IF YOU WERE to commit one recipe to memory from this book, let it be this spaghetti pomodoro. The beauty of this dish centers around the tomato, a fruit I've dedicated countless hours of my life to worshipping. The most vivid memories from my childhood come from the late summer, when my family would spend weeks preserving the ripe tomatoes we'd use for the rest of the year. To me, the tomato is so much more than an ingredient: I've slept, worked, and lived in pursuit of its greatness. This recipe is the ultimate presentation of that dedication.

Pomodoro is really a testament to the wonders of Italian cuisine: a handful of simple fresh ingredients that, when made well, dazzle. This recipe, adapted from my mother's, is what grandmothers are making in Italy at this very moment. It's what I'd eat for breakfast, lunch, and dinner. Of all the pastas in the world, this is my favorite.

Salt

⅔ cup **extra-virgin olive oil**

15 **garlic cloves,** thinly sliced

30 to 40 **basil leaves,** chopped, plus more for garnish

Pinch of **red chile flakes**

2 (24.5-ounce) bottles **Mutti tomato puree** (passata)

1 pound **spaghetti**

¾ cup freshly grated **Parmesan cheese**

1. Bring a large pot of generously salted water to a boil.

2. In a deep pan or soup pot, combine the olive oil and garlic. Set the pan over medium-high heat and begin to toast the garlic, making sure to break up any piles of garlic, continuously agitating the pot to ensure it cooks evenly. Add the basil and chile flakes and continue cooking until the garlic is a nice amber brown (but not burnt).

3. Now that the oil is infused, stir in the tomato puree and simmer for 10 to 15 minutes.

4. Meanwhile, add the spaghetti to the boiling water and cook to al dente according to the package directions.

5. Drain the pasta, add it to the pan with the pomodoro sauce, and stir until coated.

6. Serve garnished with the Parmesan and some basil.

Penne alla Vodka

I DIDN'T even taste vodka sauce, perhaps one of the most beloved Italian American dishes of all time, until I was an adult—my mother would only cook the traditional dishes from her childhood growing up in Italy. To this day, Americans can't seem to get enough of penne alla vodka, an adoration I grew to understand once I became a cook and tasted it for the first time.

This dish is an adaptation of a recipe I learned while working at Pietro's in Manhattan, where I spent my weekends earning money while I was going to culinary school. The trick? Vodka's high alcohol content makes it an adept emulsifier, boiling off quickly, imparting little of its own flavor, and allowing the heavy cream and acidic tomato to harmonize. It's this emulsification that creates the velvety texture that makes vodka sauce so delicious, and so famous.

Salt

1 pound **penne** or **rigatoni pasta**

Extra-virgin olive oil

4 **garlic cloves**, sliced

1 **shallot**, finely diced

8 **basil leaves**, coarsely chopped

Pinch of **red chile flakes**

6 ounces **tomato paste** (¾ cup)

¼ cup **vodka**

¾ cup **heavy cream**

½ cup finely grated **Parmesan cheese**

3 tablespoons **unsalted butter**

1. Bring a large pot of lightly salted water to a boil. Add the pasta and cook to al dente according to the package directions. Scoop out ½ cup of the pasta water, drain the pasta, and set aside.

2. Meanwhile, heat a large deep sauté pan over medium-high heat. Once hot, add enough olive oil to cover the bottom of the pan. Add the garlic and toast in the oil until golden.

3. Add the shallot and cook until softened and translucent. Add the basil and chile flakes and cook until fragrant. Stir in the tomato paste and cook just until it begins to caramelize, 2 to 3 minutes.

4. Reduce the heat and make a small well in the center of the pan. Slowly add the vodka, being careful not to cause any flare-ups. Let the vodka reduce by half in the well, then stir to combine.

5. Whisk in the heavy cream and the reserved pasta cooking water. Bring to a boil, then remove from the heat. Add the drained pasta, Parmesan, and butter to the pot of hot sauce and toss until fully incorporated.

Linguine Vongole, *NYC-Style*

MY MOM always did the shopping growing up, except when it came to clams: My father was charged with handling the fish market—likely because it was perceived to be a rougher crowd and they needed a grumpy old Italian man to do the job. He may have made a few enemies in the process, but he always came home with the best seafood at the lowest possible price.

This dish reminds me of those days when my father brought home a bag of shellfish and my mom made linguine vongole with her famous crushed garlic: simple, quick, and delicious.

To save time, ask your local fishmonger for preshucked cherrystones (perhaps you should avoid my father's negotiating tactics in this case). If you *do* want to take on the challenge of shucking them yourself, maybe as a fun activity with a friend, a trick I love is soaking the clams in water and sprinkling them with cornmeal or baking soda. The clams open slightly and spit out any sand that may be trapped inside.

One final tip before you get to it: This dish comes together quickly, so make sure to measure your ingredients before you get started. The last thing you want to do is overcook the clams and toughen their naturally perfect texture.

Salt

12 ounces **linguine**

Extra-virgin olive oil

12 **garlic cloves,**
peeled and whole

½ teaspoon
red chile flakes

1. Bring a large pot of generously salted water to a boil. Add the linguine and cook to al dente according to the package directions. Scoop out 1 cup of the pasta water, drain the linguine, and set aside.

2. Meanwhile, to build the sauce, first up: my mom's garlic. Set a sauté pan over medium heat. Once hot, add enough olive oil to thinly coat the bottom of the pan, then add the garlic. When the garlic starts to sizzle, crush it slightly with the back of a spoon.

3. Add the chile flakes and toast for a few seconds in the oil. Be careful to stir and adjust the heat as necessary to avoid burning.

-recipe & ingredients continue-

6 ounces **cherrystone clam meat** (from about 1½ pounds unshucked clams), coarsely chopped

½ cup **clam juice** (from your fishmonger or all-natural bottled)

¾ cup **white wine**

24 **Manila clams,** scrubbed clean and held in cool water

1 tablespoon **garlic puree**

⅛ teaspoon **ground white pepper**

1 **lemon,** halved

2 tablespoons chopped **fresh parsley,** plus more for garnish

2 tablespoons chopped **fresh chives,** plus more for garnish

4. Add the chopped cherrystone clam meat and sear without moving for a moment. When the clams start releasing their water, stir to avoid sticking.

5. Add the clam juice, wine, and Manila clams. Cover and cook until the clams open, 2 to 3 minutes.

6. Add the garlic puree, stir to combine, and season with the white pepper.

7. Squeeze the lemon over the top. Add the parsley, chives, and drained pasta and stir to combine. Adjust the consistency of the sauce with some of the reserved pasta water as needed. The sauce should coat the pasta well and not leave a puddle in the bowl.

8. Serve garnished with more parsley and chives.

Penne *with Zucchini & Sun-Dried Tomatoes*

THE UNBELIEVABLE TRUTH about Italian cooking is that your life can be forever altered with just twenty minutes and a few simple ingredients. This dish, which I've adapted from the traditional spaghetti alla Nerano, is a perfect case in point! First created by Chef Maria Grazia, who served her signature zucchini pasta in the idyllic village of Nerano on the Amalfi Coast, this version stays close to the original, with zucchini, a rather flavorless vegetable on its own, caramelized until the flavor intensifies to what can only be described as transformative.

Salt

⅓ cup **extra-virgin olive oil**

3 **garlic cloves**, sliced

3 **zucchini**, halved lengthwise and cut crosswise into half-moons

1 cup oil-packed **sun-dried tomatoes**, drained and chopped

10 **basil leaves**, chopped, plus more for garnish

⅛ teaspoon **red chile flakes**

1 cup bottled **tomato puree** (passata)

1 pound **penne pasta**

3 tablespoons **unsalted butter**

½ cup grated **Parmesan cheese**, plus more for garnish

1. Bring a large pot of generously salted water to a boil.

2. Meanwhile, set a deep sauté pan over medium-high heat. Once hot, add the olive oil and garlic and toast until the garlic is golden brown. Add the zucchini and sauté until it's lightly browned.

3. Add the sun-dried tomatoes, basil, and chile flakes and cook for 2 to 3 minutes. Stir in the tomato puree, reduce the heat to low, and simmer, stirring occasionally, while you cook the penne.

4. Add the penne to the boiling water and cook to al dente according to the package directions.

5. Drain the pasta and add it to the pan of sauce. Add the cold butter and Parmesan and stir until emulsified.

6. Serve garnished with basil and Parmesan.

OG Spaghetti Carbonara

CARBONARA is thought to get its name from carbonaro, meaning "coal burner," as it was historically made to sustain Italian charcoal workers during long hours. Though traditionally made with just four ingredients— pasta, guanciale, pecorino, and egg—it makes a quick, hearty, and satisfying dish, especially on a cold winter night. Plus, it's incredibly luxurious, considering how easily it comes together.

Salt

1 pound **spaghetti**

6 ounces **guanciale,** skin removed, sliced

12 large **egg yolks**

2 cups freshly grated **Pecorino Romano cheese**

Freshly cracked black pepper

1. Bring a large pot of lightly salted water to a boil. Add the spaghetti and cook to al dente according to the package directions.

2. Meanwhile, in a dry sauté pan, sauté the guanciale over medium heat until it's translucent and tender, about 8 minutes.

3. In a large bowl (large enough to hold the cooked pasta), whisk together the egg yolks and Pecorino Romano. Have the bowl at the ready.

4. When the pasta is almost cooked, use tongs to remove it from the water and add it to the egg yolk/pecorino mixture, allowing the pasta water to cling to the pasta. Toss until the sauce is thick and creamy.

5. Divide among four serving plates and top with the guanciale and its rendered fat. Season with several twists of pepper.

1. Mix cheese and egg yolk in a bowl. **2.** Add hot pasta directly from the pot to cheese and egg. **3.** Add more cheese.
4. Top with guanciale. **5 & 6.** Serve on four plates.

Mama Nicolina's Cavatelli
with Broccoli Rabe & Sweet Sausage

CAVATELLI, meaning "little hollows," has a hollow center and ridged texture that's perfect for sopping up as much delicious sauce as a single pasta can possibly manage—it gets gloriously lost in all the nooks and crannies. This recipe was part of my Mama Nicolina's weekly rotation. The natural bitterness of broccoli rabe is transformed with a quick blanching and plenty of garlic. The final flavor is nutty and mild, a lovely match for sweet Italian sausage and a simple butter, red chile, and Parmesan sauce.

Salt

1½ pounds **broccoli rabe**

¼ cup **extra-virgin olive oil**

1½ pounds **sweet Italian sausage**, casings removed

6 **garlic cloves**, thinly sliced

Pinch of **red chile flakes**

1 pound **cavatelli**

5 tablespoons cold **unsalted butter**

½ cup finely grated **Parmesan cheese**, plus more for garnish

1. Bring a large pot of generously salted water to a boil. Blanch the broccoli rabe in the boiling water until fork-tender, about 1 minute. Drain and run under cold water to stop the cooking process. Once cooled, squeeze out any excess water, chop into bite-size pieces, and set aside.

2. Fill the stockpot with fresh water. Bring to a boil and generously season with salt.

3. In a deep sauté pan, heat the olive oil over medium-high heat and cook the sausage, breaking it up, until it is lightly caramelized, about 10 minutes.

4. Add the garlic and chile flakes and sauté until aromatic. Add the broccoli rabe, reduce the heat to low, and let simmer while you cook the pasta.

5. Add the cavatelli to the boiling water and cook to al dente according to the package directions. Scoop out 1 cup of the pasta water, drain the pasta, and set aside.

6. Add ¾ cup of the pasta water to the pan with the sausage and broccoli rabe and stir to deglaze. Add the butter and Parmesan and stir until the sauce is emulsified.

7. Add the pasta to the sauce and stir to coat. If the sauce is too thick, add the remaining ¼ cup pasta water to thin. Serve garnished with more Parmesan.

Rigatoni White Bolognese

THIS TOMATO-FREE adaptation of the classic packs on flavor quickly with a few contemporary adjustments. Smoky bacon adds richness in minutes, and a quick braise with white wine and a touch of cream replaces the traditional slow simmer.

Salt and **freshly ground black pepper**

Extra-virgin olive oil

2 slices **bacon,** cut crosswise into strips ½ inch wide

2 **celery stalks,** finely diced

2 small **carrots,** finely diced

½ medium **yellow onion,** finely diced

2 **bay leaves**

½ cup **white wine**

2 cups **chicken stock**

½ cup **heavy cream**

1 pound **ground turkey**

8 ounces large **rigatoni**

1 tablespoon **chicken demi-glace** or **rich chicken stock**

2 tablespoons **unsalted butter**

1 cup freshly grated **Parmesan cheese**

2 tablespoons chopped **fresh parsley**

1. Bring a large pot of generously salted water to a boil.

2. In a large sauté pan, heat a dash of olive oil over medium heat. Add the bacon and render for 3 minutes. Add the celery, carrots, onion, and bay leaves. Sauté for 1 minute, then cover and allow to braise for 5 minutes.

3. Uncover, add the wine, and cook until the pan is almost dry. Add the stock. Season with ¼ teaspoon of black pepper and 2 teaspoons salt and cook for another 3 minutes. Remove the bay leaves. Stir in the cream.

4. Meanwhile, in a separate pan, heat 2 tablespoons olive oil over medium-high heat until shimmering. Add the ground turkey, use a wooden spoon to break it up, and cook until lightly browned, about 10 minutes.

5. Add the turkey to the cream mixture and stir to combine.

6. Add the rigatoni to the boiling water and cook to al dente according to the package directions. Drain the pasta and add it to the turkey and cream sauce.

7. Stir in the chicken demi-glace, butter, Parmesan, and parsley and serve.

Advanced Settings
Parsley Fregola *with Clams*

I LOVE THIS TECHNIQUE for easily preparing fresh pasta at home. Thought to have originated on the island of Sardinia, fregola has been a staple of Sardinian cuisine for centuries. The method of making it is similar to that of German spaetzle, where a soft dough is pushed through a colander into boiling water, resulting in small pasta dumplings that resemble Israeli couscous in both shape and texture. Sweet, tender clams go perfectly with the parsley-flavored dumplings. Ask your fishmonger for fresh clam juice, but if they don't have it, you can buy the all-natural bottled variety.

FREGOLA

Salt

2 cups **gluten-free all-purpose flour**

1 cup **powdered egg whites**

Freshly ground black pepper

1¾ cups **water**

Leaves from 1 bunch **parsley**

TO MAKE THE FREGOLA

1. Bring a large pot of salted water to a boil. (Choose a pot over which you can suspend a metal colander above the boiling water.)

2. Meanwhile, in a bowl, combine the flour and powdered egg whites. Season with a pinch each of salt and pepper and mix until well incorporated.

3. In a blender, combine the water and parsley leaves and blend to a fine puree. Add the flour mixture in two parts and blend until well combined and smooth with no lumps.

4. Place a metal colander on top of the pot of boiling water and turn off the heat (the size of the fregola will vary slightly depending on your colander, but the holes in most any standard colander will do—so long as you're making small pasta dumplings). Pour the mixture out of the blender into the colander and use a rubber spatula to push the dough through the holes into the just-boiled water. Allow the fregola to cook until they float, 3 to 4 minutes. Drain in a clean colander.

SAUCE

¼ cup **extra-virgin olive oil**

2 **garlic cloves,** finely sliced

⅛ teaspoon **red chile flakes**

½ cup chopped **clam meat**

½ cup **white wine**

1 cup **clam juice,** fresh or all-natural bottled

6 to 8 **Manila clams** (unshucked)

1 tablespoon chopped **fresh parsley**

TO MAKE THE SAUCE

5. In a large skillet, heat the olive oil and garlic over medium heat until evenly browned. Add the chile flakes and chopped clams and stir to coat in the oil. Cook, stirring continuously, for about 1 minute. Add the white wine and cook until reduced by half.

6. Add the clam juice and Manila clams, cover, and cook until the clams open, about 2 to 3 minutes.

7. Reduce the heat to low and add the fregola and parsley. Stir to combine, then cook for about 1 minute.

Fully Loaded Mac & Cheese

HOMEMADE mac and cheese typically starts with making a béchamel, one of the five classic mother sauces of French cuisine. From there, cheese is incorporated to make a Mornay sauce, which is then turned into a baked noodle casserole. I bridge the gap between the homemade ordeal and boxed mac and cheese with a secret ingredient—creamy Velveeta cheese, which yields a similar texture to the Mornay sauce with a fraction of the time and effort. The addition of sweet Italian sausage, cherry peppers, and pickled jalapeños gives this mac a personal twist and an extra home-cooked feeling.

Salt

1 pound **bacon,** cut crosswise into strips ½ inch wide

1 pound **sweet Italian sausage,** casings removed

1½ cups **heavy cream**

1 (4-ounce) pouch **Velveeta cheese sauce**

4 ounces **smoked provolone cheese,** rind peeled, grated

¼ cup grated **Parmesan cheese**

2 cups shredded **cheddar cheese** (8 ounces)

1. Preheat the oven to 350°F.

2. Bring a large stockpot of generously salted water to a boil. Line a large plate with paper towels.

3. In a sauté pan, cook the bacon over medium heat until it's about to brown, about 5 minutes. Scoop the cooked bacon onto the paper towels to drain.

4. Drain off half the bacon fat, then add the sausage to the pan. Use a wooden spoon to break it into bite-size pieces and cook until browned, about 10 minutes. Set aside.

5. Make a double boiler by placing a small pot filled halfway with water over medium heat. Set a heatproof bowl over the pot and bring the water to a simmer. Add the cream, Velveeta cheese sauce, provolone, Parmesan, and 1 cup of the cheddar to the bowl. Stir to combine and heat until melted.

-recipe & ingredients continue-

1 pound medium **pasta shells**

½ teaspoon **onion powder**

½ teaspoon **garlic powder**

Pinch of **cayenne pepper**

Freshly ground black pepper

¼ cup chopped mild **sweet cherry peppers**

¼ cup chopped **pickled jalapeños**

1 cup sliced **scallions**

6. Meanwhile, add the pasta shells to the boiling water and cook to al dente according to the package directions.

7. When the cheese sauce has melted, reduce the heat and stir in the onion powder, garlic powder, cayenne, and salt and black pepper to taste.

8. Drain the pasta and return it to the cooking pot. Stir in the bacon, sausage, cheese sauce mixture, cherry peppers, pickled jalapeños, and half the scallions.

9. Pour the mixture into a large cast-iron skillet, top with the remaining 1 cup cheddar, and bake until the top is golden brown, about 10 minutes.

10. Serve garnished with the remaining scallions.

American Fettuccine Chicken Alfredo

ALL DUE CREDIT goes to Italian chef Alfredo di Lelio for the first iteration of this dish, which became an Italian American classic. As the story goes, di Lelio originally conceived of a dish of *fettuccine al burro* (pasta with butter) while struggling to feed his wife after the birth of their first child. He added triple the amount of butter, which, turns out, is a pretty good trick of the trade to make your wife—or just about anyone—eat up. Americans have since adapted Lelio's famous dish with the addition of heavy cream and, often, chicken, as it's served here. Rich and indulgent, fettuccine Alfredo is one of those dishes your guests, children, wife, in-laws, and the entire neighborhood is sure to adore.

2½ pounds **boneless, skinless chicken breasts,** sliced into thin cutlets

Salt and **freshly ground black pepper**

Extra-virgin olive oil

1 stick (4 ounces) **unsalted butter**

1½ cups **heavy cream**

1½ cups grated **Parmesan cheese**

1 pound **dried fettuccine**

2 tablespoons chopped **fresh parsley**

1. Season the chicken with salt and pepper.

2. Heat a sauté pan over medium-high heat. Once hot, add enough oil to cover the bottom of the pan. Add the chicken and sear until cooked through and golden brown. When cool enough to handle, slice into 2-inch strips and set aside.

3. Bring a large stockpot of generously salted water to a boil.

4. Meanwhile, in a deep sauté pan, melt the butter over medium-high heat and cook, stirring frequently, until the butter starts to smell toasty and has small golden brown specks, 5 to 8 minutes. Add the cream and simmer until the liquid has reduced by half, then stir in the chicken and Parmesan.

5. Add the fettuccine to the boiling water and cook to al dente according to the package directions. Scoop out 1 cup of the pasta water, then drain the pasta and return it to the cooking pot.

6. Add the sauce to the pasta and toss to combine, adding some of the reserved pasta water if the sauce is too thick.

7. Serve garnished with the parsley.

Pad Thai, *Jet Tila–Style*

THOUGH its true origins are hotly contested, pad Thai has become the most undeniably well-known street food of Thailand since it was first introduced in the 1930s—a relatively recent addition to the world of classic dishes. Sweet, salty, and bright, pad Thai is the single noodle dish to satisfy just about every craving.

The not-so-secret trick to building tons of flavor very quickly in pad Thai is the fish sauce, which is made by coating fish or krill in salt and allowing them to ferment in giant barrels for at least two months. The fermentation gives the resulting liquid a naturally high glutamate content, adding an addictive umami flavor wherever it's used. While fish sauce is a beloved flavor booster for most any chef, my favorite ingredient here is the preserved radish, which adds a sour, sweet, and spicy layer to the noodles.

Get your ingredients ready before your start cooking: This dish is best made quickly over high heat.

7 ounces **pad Thai noodles**

¼ cup **fish sauce**

¼ cup **sugar**

3 tablespoons **tamarind puree** (concentrate)

1 tablespoon **fresh lime juice**

1 tablespoon **rice vinegar**

1 tablespoon **sriracha sauce**

1. Soak the noodles in lukewarm water for 30 minutes while you prepare the other ingredients.

2. In a small bowl, mix the fish sauce, sugar, tamarind puree, lime juice, vinegar, and sriracha. Set aside.

-recipe & ingredients continue-

3 tablespoons **extra-virgin olive oil**

2 **garlic cloves,** minced

1 **shallot,** sliced

2 tablespoons chopped **preserved radish**

½ cup diced **extra-firm tofu**

10 **shrimp,** peeled and deveined

2 large **eggs,** beaten

3 or 4 **scallions,** cut into 1-inch lengths

¼ cup **salted roasted peanuts,** chopped

1 cup **bean sprouts**

1 **lime,** cut into wedges

3. In a large skillet, heat the olive oil over high heat. When the oil starts to smoke, add the garlic, shallot, and preserved radish and cook for a few seconds. Add the tofu and shrimp on one side of the pan and the eggs on the other. Scramble the eggs, stirring continuously. Sauté until the shrimp start to turn pink.

4. Drain the noodles, add to the pan, and cook for 1 minute. Add the fish sauce mixture and toss to coat the noodles in the sauce. Add the scallions and stir-fry until they're bright green.

5. Transfer to a large serving platter and garnish with the peanuts, bean sprouts, and lime wedges.

Three-Star Red Crab Beurre Blanc Pasta

THE BASE of this lavish dish is beurre blanc, a classic French sauce named after the white butter that does most of the heavy lifting. Legend goes that Chef Clémence Lefeuvre forgot to add the tarragon and egg yolks to her béarnaise (another mother sauce of French cuisine). Rather than start over, she discovered a velvety, mildly sweet, and tangy sauce that's a perfect match for seafood, especially full-flavored shellfish like the red crab used here. If only all our mishaps in the kitchen ended in a major contribution to the culinary world!

One important distinction to keep in mind: Béarnaise is made with warm clarified butter. For beurre blanc, it's very important that the butter be cold. The fat within warm butter will melt too quickly and make it harder to emulsify, setting you up for a broken sauce. In addition to making sure your butter is cold, add it gradually and stir constantly.

Salt

1 pound **rigatoni**

2 tablespoons minced **shallot**

Juice of 1 **lemon**

¼ cup **white wine**

⅓ cup **heavy cream**

1 stick (4 ounces) cold **unsalted butter**, cubed

1 pound **red crabmeat**

Ground white pepper (optional)

2 tablespoons chopped **fresh chives**

1. Bring a large pot of generously salted water to a boil. Add the rigatoni and cook to al dente according to the package directions. Drain and set aside.

2. Meanwhile, in a medium saucepan, stir together the shallot, lemon juice, and white wine. Reduce over medium-low heat until syrupy, about 5 minutes.

3. Season with a pinch of salt, then add the cream and bring to a simmer. Reduce the heat to low and add the butter, a few cubes at a time, stirring continuously.

4. When all the butter has been incorporated, add the crab and drained pasta and simmer, tossing until the sauce has thickened and the pasta is coated in the sauce.

5. Adjust the seasoning with salt and a dash of white pepper, if desired. Garnish with the chives and serve.

Sandwiches & Big Salads

Classic Croque Madames

A VARIATION of the croque monsieur, a classic French brasserie sandwich, the croque madame starts with the same béchamel base, sliced ham, melted Gruyère cheese, and sharp Dijon mustard, but brings an added level of richness by topping things off with a lightly fried egg. Popping up around the 1960s, it's named after the egg's resemblance to a woman's hat. To stick to French tradition, use an uncured boiled ham: It will add a savory element without being too salty and overpowering. And, make sure your bread is nice and crusty—day-old or lightly toasted works well—so it can handle all that creamy sauce without getting soggy. Perfect for a decadent brunch; serve with a lemony salad on the side and perhaps a glass of sparkling wine.

BÉCHAMEL

2½ cups **whole milk**

4 tablespoons **unsalted butter**

¼ cup **all-purpose flour**

⅛ teaspoon **freshly grated nutmeg**

⅛ teaspoon **ground white pepper**

Salt

1. Preheat the oven to 350°F.

TO MAKE THE BÉCHAMEL

2. In a small pot, heat the milk over low heat.

3. In a separate pot, melt the butter over medium-low heat. Stir in the flour and cook, stirring, for 3 minutes. Stir in the nutmeg, white pepper, and a pinch of salt.

4. Whisk in the warm milk and cook until the mixture has thickened, about 10 minutes.

-recipe & ingredients continue-

CROQUE MADAMES

Extra-virgin olive oil

4 slices
sourdough bread

2 tablespoons
Dijon mustard

8 ounces sliced
boiled ham

8 ounces **Gruyère
cheese**, shredded

2 tablespoons
unsalted butter

4 large **eggs**

Salt and **freshly
ground black pepper**

TO COOK THE CROQUE MADAMES

5. In a medium skillet, heat enough olive oil to coat the pan over medium heat. Once hot, add the bread and toast on both sides.

6. Transfer the bread to a clean work surface and smear the mustard on each slice. Layer with the ham. Spoon the béchamel over the ham and sprinkle with the Gruyère.

7. Transfer to a sheet pan and bake for 5 minutes.

8. Meanwhile, in a small skillet, melt the butter over medium heat. Once melted and hot, fry the eggs, one at time.

9. To serve, set each croque madame on a plate and top with a fried egg. Finish with salt and black pepper.

Prosciutto Crudo Panino

PROSCIUTTO CRUDO, which means "raw ham" in Italian, is often shortened to simply prosciutto in the States. Made from pig thigh that's dry-cured using just sea salt, left unsmoked, and thinly sliced, it's a milder Italian cured meat that lets the pork's natural flavor speak for itself. Here it's paired with Boursin cheese, a creamy, easily spreadable cow's cheese flavored with a variety of herbs. Feel free to experiment with different combinations from Boursin's selection of spreads: Prosciutto tastes delicious with just about everything, both savory and sweet.

4 **ciabatta rolls**

1 (5.2-ounce) package **Boursin cheese**

8 ounces sliced **prosciutto**

1 **heirloom tomato,** sliced

Salt and **freshly ground black pepper**

1 tablespoon **extra-virgin olive oil**

Simple salad, for serving

1. Preheat a panini press or heat a cast-iron skillet over medium heat.

2. Slice open the ciabatta rolls. Smear on the Boursin cheese and layer with the prosciutto.

3. Place the sandwiches into the panini press or on the skillet. Toast for 8 minutes, making sure to flip halfway if using a skillet.

4. Season the tomato slices with salt and pepper and drizzle with the olive oil.

5. Open the panini, layer with the tomato, and close. Serve with a simple salad.

Italian Subs Long Island Deli-Style

THE SUBMARINE SANDWICH, or sub for short, is thought to have been conceived by Dominic Conti, an immigrant from Montella, a small town inland from Salerno. Conti began selling the traditional Italian sandwich out of his grocery store in Paterson, New Jersey, in 1903. He named his signature sub after its resemblance to the *Fenian Ram*, a recovered submarine that was on display at New Jersey's Paterson Museum at the time.

Being an Italian American chef from Jamaica, Queens, to say I take this sando seriously would be an understatement. This is my recipe, where I've taken just a few liberties, like frying the basil for extra crispiness. I humbly present it to you as my favorite version of the classic. If you like extra crunch, you can toast the bread beforehand in 350°F oven for 15 minutes. From there, stack it high and enjoy.

¼ cup **mayo**

8 **green olives,** pitted and chopped

1 teaspoon **whole-grain mustard**

⅛ cup **red wine vinegar**

¼ cup **extra-virgin olive oil,** plus more for frying

¼ teaspoon **dried oregano**

Small pinch of **red chile flakes**

Salt and **freshly ground black pepper**

1 cup **fresh basil leaves**

1. In a small bowl, mix together the mayo, olives, and mustard and set aside.

2. In a separate bowl, whisk together the vinegar, olive oil, oregano, and chile flakes. Season the vinaigrette with salt and black pepper to taste.

3. Line a plate with paper towels. Pour ¼ inch of olive oil into a small pot and set over medium-high heat. When the oil is hot, fry the basil for less than a minute. Remove and place on the paper towels to drain, then season with salt.

1 medium **baguette**

4 jarred **pickled cherry peppers,** sliced

4 jarred **peperoncini,** sliced

4 ounces sliced **ham**

4 ounces thinly sliced **prosciutto**

4 ounces sliced **salami**

4 ounces sliced **soppressata**

4 slices **provolone cheese**

4 slices **Swiss cheese**

1 head **iceberg lettuce,** shredded

1 **tomato,** sliced

4. Slice open the baguette with a serrated knife. Drizzle with the vinaigrette (to your taste, or a couple of tablespoons per side), then spread the olive mayo on each side.

5. Layer with the cherry peppers, peperoncini, sliced meats, both cheeses, the fried basil, shredded lettuce, and tomato.

6. Drizzle more vinaigrette over the lettuce and tomato. Season again with salt and black pepper. Close the sandwich and slice into 4 equal portions.

1. Spread the olive mayo on both sides of the bread. **2.** Drizzle the lettuce and tomatoes with vinaigrette.
3. Begin adding the deli meat. **4.** Continue stacking on the cured meat in layers. **5.** Top with the cheese.
6. Place the cherry peppers and peperoncini on the cheese and close to make a sandwich.

Banh Mi Burgers

THE CLASSIC Vietnamese sandwich is named after the French bread on which it's traditionally served, *banh* meaning "bread" in Vietnamese. An early example of fusion, it was invented after the French introduced the Vietnamese to the baguette during French colonial rule in the 1860s. It was later brought to the US by Vietnamese immigrants and widely popularized in the 1980s, thanks to a food truck and fast-food chain started by Lê Văn Bá and his sons in Northern California. Today, chefs from around the country have tried their take on the sandwich, with a "Vietnamese Po'boy" even claiming first place at the annual Oak Street Po-Boy Festival in New Orleans.

Here I take the same flavor profile and ingredients and turn the banh mi into a burger, complete with homemade BBQ sauce. Far from traditional but undeniably delicious and super easy to make, it's perfect for a sunny Sunday afternoon spent grilling outdoors.

1 large **carrot**, cut into matchsticks

1 cup **rice vinegar**

BANH MI BBQ SAUCE

3 tablespoons **hoisin sauce**

3 tablespoons **rice vinegar**

1 tablespoon **fish sauce**

2 **garlic cloves**, grated

Salt

1. Heat a grill pan over medium heat.

2. In a small bowl, combine the carrots and rice vinegar and let marinate while you prepare the other ingredients.

TO MAKE THE BANH MI BBQ SAUCE

3. In a small bowl, stir together the hoisin, vinegar, fish sauce, garlic, and salt to taste.

-recipe & ingredients continue-

BURGERS

1 pound **ground pork**

2 tablespoons
minced **shallot**

1 tablespoon
minced **jalapeño**

¼ cup chopped
fresh cilantro

Salt

Olive oil spray

ASSEMBLY

1 medium **baguette**

Mayo, for spreading

Hoisin sauce,
for drizzling

¼ head **iceberg
lettuce,** shredded

Cilantro sprigs,
for garnish

TO MAKE THE BURGERS

4. In a separate bowl, combine the pork, shallot, jalapeño, cilantro, and 3 tablespoons of the BBQ sauce. Season with salt and shape into 4 patties about ¼ inch thick.

5. Spray the grill pan with oil and grill the patties until browned, then flip and brush with the BBQ sauce. Grill until browned on the second side, about 3 to 4 minutes per side.

TO ASSEMBLE THE BANH MI

6. Cut the baguette crosswise into 4 sections, then split each section open. Wipe off the grill pan with paper towels and grill the bread for a few seconds on each side.

7. Drain the carrots. Spread mayo to your taste on the toasted baguette and drizzle with some hoisin sauce. Top with a burger, the marinated carrots, shredded lettuce, and sprigs of cilantro.

Classic BLT: Bring the Bacon

THE BLT is perhaps one of the best examples of a few simple ingredients working in harmony to create one of the most iconic sandwiches of all time. The BLT first became popular after WWII, when supermarkets began carrying ingredients like fresh tomatoes no matter the season. While year-round BLTs have been popular ever since, I must campaign for waiting for summer, when heirloom tomatoes are juicy and flavorful enough to be enjoyed with just a touch of flaky salt. For a mild, delicate bread, use Pullman (aka pain de mie) sandwich bread, or opt for sourdough for an extra touch of acidity.

1 pound **thick-cut bacon**

8 slices **sourdough** or **Pullman bread**, toasted

½ cup **Kewpie mayo**, to taste

1 large **heirloom tomato**, thinly sliced

1 head **iceberg lettuce**, leaves separated

1. Preheat the oven to 350°F.

2. Spread the bacon on a sheet pan. Transfer to the oven and bake for about 10 minutes, then flip and bake until the bacon is crispy and the fat has rendered, about 5 minutes more. Transfer to paper towels to drain.

3. Lay the toasted bread on a cutting board. Spread 1 to 2 tablespoons of the mayo on each slice of bread. Layer with the tomato, bacon, and lettuce.

4. Close the sandwiches, cut in half, and serve.

100-Year Tonkatsu Sandos

TONKATSU, a deep-fried breaded pork cutlet similar to, and most likely influenced by, the schnitzel (see page 224), originated in Japan during the Meiji era in the late nineteenth century.

With creamy and soft Japanese milk bread, rich Kewpie mayo, spicy mustard, and classic Bull-Dog tonkatsu sauce, this recipe has been perfected for more than 100 years. It's precicely perfect just as it is, so I don't mess with it. Crunchy, sweet, and savory, this sando is a sure hit.

KATSU CUTLETS

12 ounces **pork loin**

Salt and **freshly ground black pepper**

2 large **eggs**

3 tablespoons **Kewpie mayo**

2 tablespoons **S&B mustard**

1 cup **all-purpose flour**

3 cups **panko bread crumbs**

Neutral oil, for frying

SANDOS

Unsalted butter

S&B mustard

8 slices **Japanese milk bread**

½ small head **green cabbage,** cored and very thinly sliced

Kewpie mayo

Bull-Dog tonkatsu sauce

2 **lemons,** cut into wedges

TO MAKE THE KATSU CUTLETS

1. Slice the fat-trimmed pork loin into medallions ¼ inch thick. Place each medallion between two pieces of plastic wrap and use a mallet to pound them into ½-inch-thick cutlets. Season with salt and pepper.

2. Set up a breading station with three shallow dishes: In one dish, beat the eggs with the mayo and mustard. Put the flour and panko in two separate dishes. Bread the cutlets, starting with the flour, then the egg mixture, and lastly the panko.

3. Pour ½ inch of oil into a deep sauté pan and heat over medium heat to 350°F.

4. Fry the breaded cutlets until golden brown, 3 to 4 minutes per side.

TO ASSEMBLE THE SANDOS

5. Spread some room-temperature butter and mustard on all the bread slices. Add the sliced green cabbage, layer katsu cutlets on half of the bread, and spread Kewpie mayo on top.

6. Drizzle tonkatsu sauce over the top to your liking and close the sandos. Cut off the crusts and slice in half or quarters. Serve with lemon wedges for squeezing on each bite.

Just Like Pat's Philly Cheesesteaks

THE FIRST CHEESESTEAK sandwich is credited to Pat and Harry Olivieri, two brothers working a hot dog stand in South Philly's Italian Market in the 1930s, who first threw grilled steak and onions in a toasted Italian roll. The brothers quickly abandoned the hot dog business and soon their signature sandwich became so popular, they were able to open a brick-and-mortar. Today, Pat's King of Steaks still operates, slinging the same steak sandwiches but with the later addition of cheese, credited to "Cocky Joe" Lorenza, one of the restaurant's managers.

Here I keep things classic, as the Philly cheesesteak is perfect as is (in fact, I spent years trying to come up with an "elevated" Philly cheesesteak that's better than the original, and it can't be done). Feel free to buy presliced rib eye to save time. Or, if you want to buy a higher-quality NY strip steak or whole rib eye and slice it yourself, simply place it in your freezer for 2 to 3 hours until firm, then use a mandoline to carefully slice the steak from top to bottom. Your butcher is a great resource for this as well, so I encourage you to delegate. Because it's hard to get a good, classic Philly cheesesteak with no added frills outside the East Coast, this recipe has brought me great comfort when I'm far away and craving a taste of home.

8 ounces **Velveeta** or **Kraft cheese sauce**

8 ounces **cheddar cheese**, grated

1 cup **heavy cream**

Salt and **freshly ground black pepper**

1. Preheat the oven to 300°F.

2. Set up a double boiler with a pot filled a little less than halfway with simmering water with a heatproof bowl set over the top. To the bowl, add the cheese sauce, cheddar cheese, and ⅔ cup of the cream. Stir until fully melted and incorporated. If the cheese sauce seems a little stiff, add more cream ¼ cup at a time until loosened. Season with salt and pepper to taste. Turn the heat to low and keep the cheese sauce warm.

-recipe & ingredients continue-

Neutral oil

1½ pounds **yellow onions**, sliced

4 (6-inch) **hero rolls**

2 pounds **NY strip** or **rib eye steak**, thinly sliced

3. In a cast-iron skillet, heat enough oil to coat the bottom of the pan over medium heat. Add the onions and slowly cook, stirring continuously, until they're caramelized and translucent, 10 to 15 minutes. Set aside.

4. Warm the rolls in the oven for about 3 minutes.

5. In a separate cast-iron skillet, heat 1 tablespoon oil over high heat. Add the steak and cook and chop the steak until caramelized, 8 to 10 minutes.

6. Remove from the heat, add the onions and half the cheese sauce, and mix.

7. Slice open the warmed rolls and divide the steak evenly among them. Top with the remaining cheese sauce and serve.

After-School Mushroom Cheesesteaks

I'LL ADMIT this is not a traditional Philly cheesesteak, but it's not trying to be (for the classic, flip back a couple pages). It's simply a deliciously melty, cheesy, and rich sandwich that's ready in minutes. The mushrooms add an earthy umami quality and the bell peppers add sweetness and pops of color. Plus, the store-bought roast beef helps this not-so-Philly cheesesteak come together quickly, perfect for after school, work, or a late night out.

1 cup **heavy cream**

1 pound **Velveeta cheese**, shredded

½ teaspoon **garlic powder**

½ teaspoon **paprika**

¼ teaspoon **chili powder**

2 tablespoons **extra-virgin olive oil**

1 pound **mushrooms**, sliced

Salt and **freshly ground black pepper**

1 **yellow onion**, diced

1 **green bell pepper**, chopped

1 **red bell pepper**, sliced

1 pound sliced **roast beef**

1 medium **baguette**

1. In a medium pot, bring the cream to a simmer over medium heat. Add the Velveeta, garlic powder, paprika, and chili powder and whisk to combine. Set aside.

2. In a sauté pan, heat the olive oil over medium-high heat. Add the mushrooms, season with salt and black pepper to taste, and sauté until golden brown. Add the onion and bell peppers and sauté until tender, about 5 minutes.

3. Shingle the roast beef into the pan and stir-fry until the beef is hot.

4. Split the baguette open. Spread half the cheese sauce on one side of the bread, then layer with the roast beef and mushroom mix, smother with more cheese sauce, and close. (You can store any leftover cheese sauce, covered, in your refrigerator, for up to 3 days. Reheat and use as a dip for chips.)

5. Slice into 4 equal pieces.

Five Trucks Shrimp Cocktail Burgers

POPULAR IN THE SOUTH, green tomatoes are simply unripe tomatoes (not to be confused with the tender green-hued heirloom tomatoes found in the summer months). Seasonality depends on where you live, but they're most abundant in late summer and early fall when farmers begin harvesting the tomatoes that didn't ripen by the end of the growing season. They're firm and not super juicy, allowing them to hold their structure over high heat. Here they're lightly breaded, fried, and served in a hamburger bun with a grilled shrimp patty. The visual is my playful modern gastronomy take on the classic shrimp cocktail. I served this photo-worthy dish at my food truck— which I often griped felt like I was running five trucks instead of one. It was all worth it for this gloriously stacked burger.

SHRIMP PATTIES

1½ pounds **shrimp, peeled and deveined**

Salt and **freshly ground black pepper**

SPICY MAYO

2 teaspoons drained **capers**

¼ cup **cornichons,** drained

1 small handful **fresh flat-leaf parsley leaves**

¼ cup canned **chipotle peppers in adobo sauce**

1 cup **mayo**

3 tablespoons **fresh lemon juice**

TO MAKE THE SHRIMP PATTIES

1. Put ½ pound of the shrimp in the food processor and process into a paste. Transfer to a separate bowl.

2. Place the remaining shrimp on a cutting board and cut each one into 6 pieces, then stir into the shrimp paste.

3. Form the shrimp mixture into 4 patties and chill in the refrigerator to firm.

TO MAKE THE SPICY MAYO

4. In the food processor, pulse the capers, cornichons, and parsley until they're coarsely chopped. Add the chipotle peppers and process until smooth. Transfer the mixture to a bowl, stir in the mayo and lemon juice, and set aside.

-recipe & ingredients continue-

FRIED GREEN TOMATOES

2 **eggs,** lightly beaten

1 cup **all-purpose flour**

1 cup **panko bread crumbs**

2 **green tomatoes,** cut into slices ¼ inch thick

Salt and **freshly ground black pepper**

Neutral oil, for shallow-frying

ASSEMBLY

Salt and **freshly ground black pepper**

Neutral oil, for the grill pan

4 **brioche hamburger buns,** split

Lettuce, torn into pieces

4 **cocktail onions**

4 **cornichons**

4 cooked **shrimp**

TO MAKE THE FRIED GREEN TOMATOES

5. Set up a breading station with three shallow dishes: one with the beaten eggs, one with the flour, and one with the panko.

6. Season the tomatoes with salt and pepper, then coat them first in the flour, then in the egg, and lastly in the panko.

7. Pour 1 inch of oil into a deep pan and heat over medium heat to about 350°F.

8. Working in batches, fry the tomatoes until golden brown, about 4 minutes per side. Set aside on paper towels to drain.

TO ASSEMBLE THE SANDWICHES

9. Heat a grill pan over high heat.

10. Season the shrimp patties with salt and pepper. Lightly oil the grill pan, add the patties, and cook until pink and firm, 3 to 4 minutes per side. The internal temperature should read about 165°F.

11. If desired, toast the buns.

12. Spread the spicy mayonnaise on the halved bun. Place a shrimp patty on each, followed by a fried tomato slice and a piece of lettuce on the bottom half of each bun, and close with the tops. On each of 4 bamboo skewers, skewer 1 cocktail onion, 1 cornichon, and 1 cooked shrimp. Stick one loaded skewer into each burger and serve.

Chopped Cheese Sandwiches, *Bronx Bodega-Style*

A NEW YORK CLASSIC, the chopped cheese can be found in bodegas across the city, with Upper Manhattan, the Bronx, and Queens having the best versions, in my opinion. Though the true origins of the chopped cheese are unclear, it's thought to be an adaptation of the Arabic dish dagha yamneeya, which is made with chopped or ground beef fried in butter, loaded with vegetables and spices, and served with Yemeni bread.

Here I break down my home recipe for the bodega chopped cheese, with a fun deviation: I love to serve mine in a flour tortilla, burrito-style. Shocking? Maybe. Delicious? Certainly.

2 tablespoons **neutral vegetable oil**

1½ pounds **ground beef** (70/30)

½ teaspoon **onion powder**

½ teaspoon **garlic powder**

½ teaspoon **paprika**

Salt and **freshly ground black pepper**

1 medium **red onion**, sliced

2 teaspoons **apple cider vinegar**

4 burrito-size **flour tortillas**

1. In a sauté pan, heat the oil over medium heat. Add the ground beef and use a wooden spoon to crumble. Cook until the meat has browned.

2. Sprinkle in the onion powder, garlic powder, paprika, and salt and pepper to taste and cook for 1 more minute. Add the red onion and sauté until the onion is translucent. Add the vinegar and adjust the seasoning to your preference. Set aside off the heat.

3. On a sheet of foil, place the tortillas over an open flame for 5 seconds on each side to soften.

4 slices
American cheese

4 slices
provolone cheese

½ head
iceberg lettuce,
shredded

1 **vine tomato,**
chopped

½ cup **mayo**

½ cup **ketchup**

2 tablespoons
unsalted butter

Tabasco sauce,
for serving

4. Lay a slice of American cheese in the middle of each tortilla. Cut a slice of provolone into 5 pieces and place a piece of provolone cheese on each edge of a tortilla—this will act as a glue.

5. Divide the beef evenly over the tortillas. Follow with the lettuce, tomato, mayo, and ketchup.

6. Fold each wrap like a burrito by tucking in the sides, then rolling up from the bottom to enclose the fillings.

7. In a separate skillet, melt the butter over medium heat. Add the wraps, seam-side down, then flip and brown on the seam side, then flip to brown the other side. Finish by wrapping the browned burritos in foil and parchment.

8. Slice the wraps in half and serve with Tabasco sauce.

1. Drizzle the beef and vegetables with mayo and ketchup. **2.** Fold in the two opposing sides, then roll and drag to make a tight wrap. Brown the wraps in butter in a medium pan, then return to the foil. **3-5.** Wrap with foil and parchment paper. **6.** Use a sharp knife to slice the wrap in half on a diagonal.

Messy True au Poivre Burgers

STEAK AU POIVRE is thought to have originated in the nineteenth century in Normandy, where diners in late-night bistros were lauding the aphrodisiac properties of the peppery sauce. Au poivre is the caramelized, salt-and-peppery outer crust of the steak—the most delicious part— concentrated in sauce form, with added cream for body and Cognac for complexity.

Here the sauce is spooned over a Gruyère cheeseburger and served on brioche with peppery fresh watercress. Tellicherry peppercorns, a larger variety with a more pungent and slightly citrusy flavor, give this sauce a nice intensity. This dish is decidedly fancier than your average burger, but just as comforting. Most restaurants use a mayonnaise version of au poivre, but I like to keep mine traditional. It may be messier, but it's true (and worth it). Grab a napkin and roll up your sleeves.

AU POIVRE SAUCE

1 tablespoon **unsalted butter**

1 tablespoon chopped **shallot**

2 tablespoons **Tellicherry peppercorns**, crushed

⅓ cup **Cognac**

¼ cup **chicken demi-glace** or **rich chicken stock**

1 cup **heavy cream**

2 **Medjool dates**, pitted and diced

1 tablespoon chopped **fresh tarragon**

TO MAKE THE AU POIVRE SAUCE

1. In a saucepan, melt the butter over medium heat. Add the shallot and sweat in the butter until translucent.

2. Add the peppercorns and cook until fragrant, then deglaze the pan with the Cognac. Reduce until almost dry.

3. Add the chicken demi-glace and simmer over medium heat for 2 minutes. Add the cream and reduce by half; keep warm over low heat. Stir in the dates, bring to a boil, and finish with the tarragon.

-recipe & ingredients continue-

BURGERS

4 slices **bacon**

1½ pounds
ground beef (75/25)

Salt and **freshly
ground black pepper**

4 slices **Gruyère** cheese

4 **brioche buns,** split

½ medium **red onion,**
thinly sliced

1 cup **watercress**

TO MAKE THE BURGERS

4. Preheat the broiler.

5. In a large sauté pan, cook the bacon over medium heat until crispy, about 10 minutes. Then set aside to drain on paper towels.

6. Heat a grill pan over medium heat.

7. Shape the meat into 4 patties. Season with salt and pepper on both sides, then grill for 5 minutes on each side.

8. Top each burger with a slice of Gruyère and place under the broiler until the cheese melts.

9. Assemble the burgers on the buns and layer with the red onion, bacon, and watercress. Smother with the au poivre sauce.

Tuna Melt to Kill For

LIKE MANY of the greatest American dishes of all time, the tuna melt is a result of some scrappy cooks making the most of what they had on hand. When last night's leftovers were mixed with mayo and scooped onto a grilled cheese for lunch service, the tuna melt was born. Here, the same premise is given a few tweaks: Olives add a briny sweetness, Dijon gives a nice kick, and pesto adds a welcome layer of flavor. The open face allows the cheese to melt, bubble, and turn golden brown with very little effort. It's just as economical and easy as the original but with a few tasty upgrades. Serve with a sharp knife and fork.

4 slices **country bread**

2 tablespoons minced **celery**

6 **Kalamata olives,** pitted and chopped

2 (5-ounce) cans **oil-packed tuna,** drained

½ cup **mayo**

1 teaspoon **Dijon mustard**

Grated zest of 1 **lemon**

2 teaspoons **fresh lemon juice**

Salt and **freshly ground black pepper**

½ cup **pesto**

1 **Roma tomato,** sliced

4 slices **provolone cheese**

1. Preheat the broiler to high.

2. Lay the bread on a sheet pan and toast under the broiler for 1 minute on each side.

3. In a medium bowl, combine the celery, olives, tuna, mayo, mustard, lemon zest, lemon juice, and salt and pepper to taste.

4. Arrange the tuna salad on the bread and layer with the pesto, tomato slices, and provolone.

5. Broil until the cheese has melted and is golden brown, 1 to 2 minutes.

6. Transfer to a cutting board and slice each tuna melt into 3 pieces.

Too-Easy Vietnamese Beef Salad

IN THIS FRESH meets deeply savory meets way-too-easy-to-be-this-good salad, sweet, bright, and umami-rich nuoc cham brings restaurant-quality flavor in mere seconds; the versatile sauce is worth stocking in your pantry. This lively salad deserves the best fruit and vegetables you can find. Make it when you find a particularly juicy mango at your store or farmers' market.

4 tablespoons **Thai-style sweet chili sauce**

1½ pounds **filet mignon** (about 1 inch thick), cut into 4 (6-ounce) portions

Salt and **freshly ground black pepper**

1 large firm **mango,** thinly sliced

1 large **seedless cucumber,** peeled, halved lengthwise, and sliced crosswise into thin half-moons

1 medium **red onion,** thinly sliced

½ cup **nuoc cham**

⅓ cup chopped **fresh cilantro**

⅓ cup chopped **fresh mint**

1 head **Boston lettuce,** leaves separated

1. Preheat a grill or broiler to high or heat a grill pan over high heat.

2. Rub 2 tablespoons of the chili sauce into the meat. Season generously with salt and pepper.

3. Grill the meat to medium-rare, about 3 minutes per side. Remove from the grill and allow to cool slightly, about 5 minutes.

4. Meanwhile, in a large bowl, toss together the remaining 2 tablespoons chili sauce, the mango, cucumber, onion, nuoc cham, cilantro, and mint.

5. Slice the beef thinly and toss gently with the mango-cucumber mixture. Season to taste with salt and pepper and serve with the lettuce leaves.

Guy's Ranch Kitchen Wedge Salad
with Smoked Brisket

IF YOU THINK of the top salads of all time, the wedge is high on the list—I imagine it up there rubbing elbows with the Caesar and the Niçoise. Just about everyone has known and loved a wedge salad in their lifetime: It's been running the show on steak house menus since the 1960s. And what's not to love? It's creamy, salty, just a touch funky, and all-around nostalgic.

I came up with this version of the classic wedge on *Guy's Ranch Kitchen*, a competition cooking show that favors ultra comfort food and outrageous eats that are perfect for devouring while watching football. I was feeling nervous about my chances: My background in fine dining and health-focused dishes isn't exactly on-brand with dishes like "Trash Can Nachos." I came up with this salad, which incorporates the best of so many worlds: wedge salad, steak house, and BBQ, all in one crowd-pleasing dish.

Smoky brisket replaces bacon, cut by a tangier, slightly more layered version of blue cheese dressing that's hard to resist eating by itself. Dill, parsley, and meaty beefsteak tomatoes hold their own in terms of flavor, adding a nice freshness to the dish. Guy not only approved, he loved it! It became a surprising staple on my own table at home, partly because it always stuns my guests, but mostly because it comes together so quickly: Pick up a smoked brisket from your local BBQ restaurant, warehouse club store, or supermarket, and the rest is easy.

-recipe continues-

2 ounces **blue cheese chunks,** plus more for garnish

6 tablespoons **sour cream**

2 tablespoons **white balsamic vinegar**

6 tablespoons **mayo**

2 tablespoons **honey**

2 tablespoons minced **fresh dill,** plus more for garnish

2 tablespoons minced **fresh parsley,** plus more for garnish

¼ cup **buttermilk**

Salt and **freshly ground black pepper**

4 heads **Bibb** or **iceberg lettuce**

2 pounds **smoked barbecue brisket**

3 **beefsteak tomatoes,** cut into wedges

1. In a bowl, combine the blue cheese chunks, sour cream, vinegar, mayo, honey, dill, parsley, buttermilk, and salt and pepper to taste.

2. Slice the lettuce into halves or quarters depending on the size. Remove any hard root ends and place on your serving plates.

3. Cube the brisket into bite-size pieces and arrange around the lettuce. Distribute the tomatoes among the plates. Dress the salad with the blue cheese dressing. Season with salt and pepper. Garnish with crumbled blue cheese and serve.

Everyday Pesto Orzo Caprese

THIS PASTA salad's roots can be traced to a crushed herb, cheese, oil, and vinegar spread served in ancient Rome. The Roman snack was later adapted in Genoa, where fresh herbs were an affordable way to add flavor when spices were still a luxury. Thus the holy grail sauce known as pesto was born, derived from pestare, meaning "to crush."

Over two thousand years later, we're still playing with variations on the original pesto sauce. Here I blanch and shock the basil and blend for a version that's nicely smooth and vibrantly green. The ciliegine works well with the cherry tomatoes' size, but if you have a beautiful ball of mozzarella on hand, feel free to cube that up instead. This summer salad goes with just about anything—a welcome addition to any picnic or potluck.

Salt

2 cups **fresh basil**, plus more for garnish

8 ounces **orzo**

¼ cup **pine nuts**

¼ cup **extra-virgin olive oil**

½ cup freshly grated **Parmesan cheese**, plus more for garnish

Freshly ground black pepper

2 cups **cherry tomatoes**, halved

8 ounces **ciliegine mozzarella**, drained

1. Set up a medium bowl of equal parts ice and water. Bring a pot of generously salted water to a boil.

2. Add the basil to the boiling water and blanch for 10 seconds, then use tongs or a sieve to transfer to the ice bath. Drain well.

3. Add the orzo to the boiling water and cook to al dente according to the package directions. Drain and set aside.

4. In a small sauté pan, toast the pine nuts over low heat until golden, about 2 minutes. Stir frequently and keep a watchful eye to avoid burning.

5. In a blender, combine the blanched basil, olive oil, 2 tablespoons of the toasted pine nuts, the Parmesan, and a pinch each of salt and pepper. Pulse until almost smooth. Taste and adjust the seasoning with more salt and pepper.

6. In a bowl, combine the orzo, cherry tomatoes, mozzarella, and pesto. Season with salt and pepper.

7. Distribute among four plates. Finish each plate with a sprinkle of toasted pine nuts, basil leaves, and more Parmesan.

Serves 4
Total Time: **20 minutes**
Ease of Preparation: **Difficult**

Summer Plunder Salad
with Tomato, Peppers, Corn & Shrimp

IN THE SUMMER months when my garden is full of fresh produce and herbs, I look forward to waking up, making an espresso, and plundering the small field I call my garden for whatever is ripe and ready. That routine became this fresh summer salad recipe. While I sadly can't grow shrimp in my backyard, their delicately sweet flavor and springy texture is well worth the trip to the market. Feel free to improvise with the vegetables that are freshest and most easily available to you.

½ cup **extra-virgin olive oil**

1 tablespoon **red wine vinegar**

Juice of 1 **lemon**

1 small **red onion,** thinly sliced

2 cups very ripe **tomatoes,** cut into wedges

3 cups cubed **day-old bread,** toasted

Salt and **freshly ground black pepper**

2 **red bell peppers**

2 ears **fresh corn**

1 pound medium-size **shrimp,** peeled and deveined

1 cup **basil leaves,** torn

1. In a large bowl, toss together the olive oil, vinegar, lemon juice, red onion, tomatoes, and bread. Season with salt and black pepper and stir. Let sit for 1 minute to allow the bread to absorb the liquid and soften.

2. Grill the bell peppers over an open flame, turning until charred and blackened on all sides, for 6 to 8 minutes in total. Place in a bowl and cover with plastic wrap. Set aside to steam until cool enough to handle, then peel off the charred skin.

3. Place the corn over an open flame and char, turning, until lightly blackened on all sides, about 8 minutes. Set aside until cool enough to handle, then trim off the top and bottom with a sharp knife. Balance the corn on one end and run your knife along the husk, removing the kernels from top to bottom.

4. Grill the shrimp over high heat, flipping until firm yet tender, about 3 to 5 minutes.

5. Add the bell peppers, corn, shrimp, and basil to the bread mixture and fold everything together. Season with additional salt and black pepper, if needed.

6. Divide among four bowls or serve family-style.

Everyday Delicious

Crudos, Simple Fish & Marinated Dishes

Tuna Avocado Furikake Crudo

RAW TUNA appears in this book repeatedly for two reasons:
1. It's delicious, and 2. it's a crowd-pleaser. After all these years, people are finally excited by raw fish, not only in restaurants but also at home. Of all the options, raw tuna, lightly cooked or chemically transformed via citrus (aka ceviche), is your best bet.

   If you can't get your hands on fresh sushi-grade tuna, use previously frozen blocks of tuna (saku tuna). And if you avoid soy, coconut aminos is a worthy substitute.

5 **limes**

¼ cup plus 2 teaspoons **extra-virgin olive oil**

2 tablespoons **soy sauce**

2 tablespoons **honey**

1 **fresh long red chile,** seeded and minced

2 tablespoons chopped **fresh cilantro leaves,** plus a few sprigs for garnish

1 **avocado,** diced

Salt

24 ounces **sushi-grade tuna**

4 teaspoons **furikake**

¼ cup **salmon roe**

1. Juice 4 of the limes into a medium bowl. Juice the fifth lime into a separate bowl.

2. To the bowl with the larger amount of juice, add ¼ cup of the olive oil, the soy sauce, honey, red chile, and chopped cilantro.

3. To the other bowl, add the avocado and remaining 2 teaspoons olive oil and gently stir together. Season with salt to taste.

4. If you're using the belly of the tuna, place it on a cutting board and use a metal spoon to separate the meat from the connective tissue. Discard any fibrous sinew. Chop the flesh into small cubes, then mince any odds and ends.

5. Add the tuna to the bowl with the soy sauce mixture and gently fold. Adjust the seasoning with salt.

6. Set out four serving plates. Place one-quarter of the diced avocado mixture on each plate. Scoop one-quarter of the tuna mixture over the avocado.

7. Repeat for the remaining three plates.

8. Sprinkle the top of each tartare with the furikake, cilantro sprigs, and salmon roe. Serve immediately.

Shrimp Cocktail
with Spicy Chili Mayo

FOR A SUREFIRE dish everyone will love, few do the job quite like shrimp cocktail. I love this take on the classic, which swaps cocktail sauce for a spicy "chili mayo," a combination of Kewpie mayo (a richer, smoother mayonnaise from Japan) and sambal oelek (a thicker, sugar-free sriracha from Indonesia). It's the perfect balance of something new paired with something super nostalgic. Plus, if you're in a rush or can't be bothered, poached shrimp are sold in just about every grocery store.

4 cups **water**

1 **celery stalk,** halved

½ medium **red onion**

1 **garlic clove,** peeled and whole

¼ teaspoon **ground fennel seeds**

½ teaspoon **seafood seasoning**

1 **bay leaf**

1 teaspoon **black peppercorns**

1 **lemon,** cut into wedges

1 pound **shrimp,** peeled and deveined

½ cup **Kewpie mayo**

¼ cup **ketchup**

1 tablespoon **sambal oelek**

1 teaspoon **apple cider vinegar**

1. In a medium pot, combine the water, celery stalk, red onion, garlic, fennel, seafood seasoning, bay leaf, peppercorns, and half the lemon wedges. Bring to a boil over high heat and boil for 10 minutes. Use a small metal sieve to remove the solids from the poaching liquid, leaving the liquid in the pot.

2. Meanwhile, make an ice bath by adding equal parts ice and water to a large bowl.

3. Bring the poaching liquid back to a boil and add the shrimp. Cook the shrimp until they turn pink, about 1 minute, then transfer to the ice bath to cool.

4. In a small bowl, whisk together the mayo, ketchup, sambal, and vinegar until combined.

5. Chill the shrimp and chili mayo until you're ready to serve. Plate the shrimp by hanging them around the rim of a glass. Dollop the chili mayo in the middle of the glass.

6. Serve with the remaining lemon wedges on the side.

Crab & Heirloom Tomato Salad *with Super-Sweet Corn Broth*

I ADAPTED this vibrant salad from my book *Flavor,* maintaining its total celebration of summer's best produce with one welcome addition: fresh crab. Garlic-infused oil, basil-scented vinegar, sweet fresh corn broth, and salty, creamy crab meld together for a truly magical experience. The result is an elevated first course, perfect for any dinner party or weeknight celebration.

While many of these ingredients can be found in grocery stores year-round, this salad in particular rewards patience. Wait until the peak of summer, when the corn is extra sweet, and the tomatoes are thriving.

1½ bunches **Thai basil**, leaves chopped and stems cut to 1-inch pieces

¼ cup **red wine vinegar**

Salt

3 ears **corn**, husked and halved crosswise

2 teaspoons **sugar** (optional)

Freshly ground black pepper

8 **garlic cloves**, peeled and whole

1 cup **extra-virgin olive oil**

4 **heirloom tomatoes**

8 ounces **lump crabmeat**

4 ounces **goat cheese**

1. In a small bowl, cover the basil stems with the red wine vinegar. Add ½ teaspoon salt and set aside.

2. Grate the corn on the large holes of a box grater. Place the kernels in a saucepan along with the cobs and just enough water to cover. Simmer for 10 minutes, then discard the cobs and pass the broth through a fine-mesh sieve into a bowl. Taste the corn broth for sweetness and add the sugar, if desired, then season with salt and pepper.

3. Meanwhile, bring a small saucepan of water to a boil. Add the garlic and boil for 1 minute. Drain the water and return the garlic to the saucepan. Add the olive oil, set the pan over medium-low heat, and simmer until the garlic has infused the oil and is aromatic, about 6 minutes. Remove from the heat.

-recipe continues-

4. Place the tomatoes over an open flame on your stovetop. Use tongs to rotate until the tomatoes are blistered on all sides. Set the tomatoes aside until they're cool enough to handle, then peel and slice into thick rounds.

5. In a glass container, combine the tomatoes and chopped basil leaves. Season with salt and pepper, then strain the garlic oil over the top (you can reserve the confit garlic cloves for a future recipe).

6. Pull the tomatoes from their marinade, letting any excess oil drip off. Arrange on four individual plates.

7. Whisk the leftover tomato marinade into the sweet corn broth to make a sauce.

8. Place the crabmeat in a medium bowl and drizzle with a touch of the sauce. Stir gently to combine.

9. Top the tomatoes with the crabmeat and drizzle with more sauce.

10. Strain the basil stems out of the vinegar (and discard the basil stems). Splash each plate with the vinegar. Crumble the goat cheese over the top of each salad and serve.

Spicy Salmon Salad (Not TikTok)

CRISPY FRIED SHALLOTS and a creamy, sweet-meets-spicy sauce make this fresh salmon salad quite popular. Though I promise this one's better than the TikTok version! This light yet comforting dish won't last long on your table. In fact, you're almost sure to find this same exact salad at your local sushi restaurant: It's an easy hit.

There's a lot of opportunity to get creative with this recipe. The chili sauce is very mildly spicy, so give it a taste and add more sriracha according to your tolerance. Serve over steamed rice for a fun take on a rice bowl or serve the rice on the side with some freshly toasted nori for a deconstructed sushi roll.

Fried Shallots (page 108)

1 pound **sushi-grade salmon,** skinned

½ cup **mayo**

2 tablespoons **sriracha sauce**

2 teaspoons **ketchup**

1 teaspoon **toasted sesame oil**

Salt

2 tablespoons **furikake**

½ **English cucumber,** diced

2 handfuls of **salad greens**

1. Make the fried shallots as directed and set aside.

2. Mince the salmon with a sharp knife or in a food processor (if you're using a food processor, be very careful not to overprocess).

3. In a large bowl, mix the mayo, sriracha, ketchup, sesame oil, and salt to taste. Fold the minced salmon into the sriracha mixture.

4. Plate the salmon and top with the fried shallots and furikake. Serve alongside the cucumber and salad greens.

Curry Kani Salad

THE WORD KANI in "kani salad" (a mayo-based dish popular in Japan) is short for kani kama, the imitation crab sticks used by Japanese sushi restaurants. Kani kama is a great back-pocket ingredient, not only because it's available year-round, but also because it's made of finfish rather than crab, which makes it perfect for serving a crowd while accommodating crustacean allergies or kosher diets.

As with many mayo-based salads, the addition of the slightly spicy Madras curry here brings the flavor to the next level. If you're a big fan of curry, take things up a notch by toasting the spices in a small sauté pan for a minute or two until aromatic before stirring them into the mayo.

1 pound **imitation crab**, shredded

2 tablespoons sliced **scallions**

¼ cup minced **celery**

1 **apple**, cored and cut into matchsticks

¼ cup **raisins**, soaked in warm water for 10 minutes and drained

1 cup **mayo**

1 teaspoon **Madras curry powder**, plus more if needed

Juice of **1 lime**, plus more if needed

2 tablespoons **salted roasted peanuts**

2 tablespoons minced **fresh tarragon**

Salt

8 **Boston lettuce leaves**

1. In a large bowl, combine the imitation crab, scallions, celery, apple, raisins, mayo, curry powder, lime juice, coarsely chopped peanuts, and tarragon. Season with a pinch of salt.

2. Taste and adjust the seasoning with more salt, lime juice, and curry powder to your preference. Serve with the lettuce leaves.

Kitchen-Sink Crudo
with Chicharrones

RAW FISH has become as ubiquitous on modern menus as molten chocolate cake was in the early 2000s. As a fan since the fourth grade, I couldn't be more ready. Far from the raw fish phobia of the past century when sushi first made its debut in America, crudo styles from all around the world are now in high demand. People have embraced—and perhaps even fallen hard for—seasoned and marinated raw fish and seafood in all its many delicious forms.

I've been eating, creating, and putting crudos on menus since I became a chef. I love serving them for dinner at home because they're simple, fast, and delicious. This version is a nice culmination of that history: It combines many of my favorite flavors and regional influences from my time in professional kitchens and playing around at home. It's got a lot going on, and that's intentional—it's everything I love to keep in my kitchen (minus the sink, as the saying goes). Feel free to improvise with the flavors and ingredients that make you happy and are easily available to you.

CRUDO

1 **jalapeño**, thinly sliced

¼ cup **fresh lime juice** (from about 2 limes)

12 ounces **sushi-grade tuna**, sliced into thin squares

4 ounces **bay scallops**, **halibut**, or **fatty salmon**, sliced into thin squares

2 tablespoons sliced **peperoncini** and ¼ cup **pickling liquid** from the jar

TO ASSEMBLE THE CRUDO

1. In a large nonreactive bowl, marinate the jalapeño in the lime juice for 10 minutes.

2. Add the tuna, scallops, peperoncini and their pickling liquid, Calabrian chiles and their oil, tomato, cilantro, and 1 teaspoon salt. Toss to combine, season to taste, and set aside.

-recipe & ingredients continue-

2 **Calabrian chiles in oil**, sliced, plus 1 tablespoon **oil** from the jar

1 large **tomato**, peeled, cored, and finely diced

½ cup **fresh cilantro leaves**, coarsely chopped

Sea salt

Neutral oil, for frying

2 tablespoons drained **capers**

1 cup thinly sliced **shallots**

½ cup **cornstarch**

Sea salt

½ cup **mayo**

2 teaspoons **fresh lime juice**

2 teaspoons **yuzu juice** or **yuzu hot sauce**, plus more if needed

1 teaspoon **yuzu kosho**

1 teaspoon **honey**

½ cup **pork chicharrones**, crumbled

½ cup **extra-virgin olive oil**

TO FINISH

3. Line a tray with paper towels. Pour 1 inch of oil into a deep pot and heat over medium heat to 350°F.

4. Add the capers to the hot oil and fry until they're crispy, about 2 minutes. Use a small metal sieve to transfer them to the paper towels to drain.

5. Toss the shallots with the cornstarch and drop them into the hot oil. Stir continuously until the shallots are crisp and about to turn golden brown, about 3 minutes. Use the sieve to transfer the shallots to the paper towels with the capers. Season with salt.

6. In a medium bowl, mix the mayo, lime juice, yuzu juice, yuzu kosho, honey, and a pinch of salt. Adjust the seasoning with more yuzu juice and salt to taste.

7. To serve, place a dollop of the yuzu mayo on each of four serving plates. Layer with the crudo. Top the crudo with chicharrones, capers, and fried shallots. Drizzle with the olive oil and serve.

The Ceviche
con *Leche de Tigre Edita Made Me*

A SPICY MARINADE for curing fish, leche de tigre, or "tiger's milk," breaks every cooking rule I've ever learned, yet it is so unbelievably tasty. I learned about it from my Peruvian friend Edita, who makes the best ceviche I've ever had—she taught me her recipe, and I'm still working to make it as well as she does. The creamy, citrusy broth is absolutely packed with aromatic deliciousness. Poured directly over sweet, flaky fluke while still hot, it gently cooks the fish to tender perfection. The result is a flavor bomb you won't believe you made in your home kitchen in just 15 minutes. This recipe is also super versatile: Feel free to use any chile, citrus, and fish you have on hand.

2 cups **water**

4 sprigs **cilantro**

⅛ teaspoon **seafood seasoning**

2 tablespoons **evaporated milk**

1 pound **fluke,** thinly sliced

½ medium **red onion,** thinly sliced

1 **fresh Thai chile**

1 (¼-inch) piece **fresh ginger,** peeled and sliced

1 (2-inch) piece **celery,** sliced

3 tablespoons **fresh lemon juice**

1 **garlic clove,** peeled and whole

Salt

1. In a small pot, combine the water, cilantro, seafood seasoning, evaporated milk, and a slice of the fluke. Bring to a simmer over medium-high heat, then adjust the heat to maintain a simmer and cook for 10 minutes.

2. Meanwhile, arrange the remaining fluke slices on a large serving platter and scatter the red onion slices over the top.

3. Place the Thai chile over an open flame on your stovetop. Use tongs to rotate until charred on all sides, about 2 minutes. Remove the stem.

4. When the fish broth is ready, pour the contents of the pot into a blender. Add the charred chile, ginger, celery, lemon juice, garlic, and salt to taste. Blend until pureed and smooth. This is the leche de tigre.

5. Pour the hot leche de tigre over the fish. Transfer to the fridge to marinate for 20 minutes.

6. Serve chilled.

Shrimp Ceviche,
Robert's Mother's Style

MY FASCINATION with ceviche goes way back to Robert, my childhood best friend and neighbor, who was like a brother to me growing up. You see, my mom was very strict with what we could eat—she didn't like us experimenting with food other than the dishes she cooked. Then came Robert, who was adopted as part of the family. When my mom became his godmother, she began making exceptions, and I was permitted to try the Ecuadorian food Robert's family cooked. His mom's ceviche completely blew my mind. I like to think of it as divine intervention.

This is a classic ceviche, inspired by that first one I ever tried, with a few tweaks: Where South and Central American ceviche is typically "cooked" in citrus juice, I first gently poach the shrimp in a flavorful liquid for a soft, supple texture and a milder flavor. A touch of ketchup adds a nice sweetness, perfect for pleasing a wide variety of palates. Serve with plenty of crispy tostadas or fresh lettuce spears for scooping.

4 cups **water**

1 **celery stalk**, halved

½ medium **red onion**

3 **garlic cloves**, peeled and whole

½ teaspoon **seafood seasoning**

¼ teaspoon **ground fennel seeds**

1 **bay leaf**

1 teaspoon **black peppercorns**

½ **lemon**, sliced

1. In a medium pot, combine the water, celery, ¼ red onion (save the remaining ¼ onion for later), 1 garlic clove, the seafood seasoning, fennel, bay leaf, peppercorns, and lemon. Bring to a boil over high heat and boil for 10 minutes. Use a small metal sieve to remove the solids from the poaching liquid, leaving the liquid in the pot.

2. Meanwhile, make an ice bath by adding equal parts ice and water to a large bowl.

1 pound **shrimp,** peeled and deveined

1 **fresh long red chile,** thinly sliced

¼ cup **fresh cilantro leaves,** chopped

3 tablespoons **ketchup**

Juice of 2 **limes**

Salt

Lettuce spears, for serving

3. Bring the poaching liquid back to a boil and add the shrimp. Cook the shrimp until they turn pink, about 1 minute, then transfer to the ice bath to cool. Once cool, pat dry and dice.

4. Thinly slice the remaining ¼ red onion and add to a medium bowl. Finely grate in the remaining 2 garlic cloves. Add the diced shrimp, red chile, cilantro, ketchup, and lime juice and season with salt. Cover and refrigerate for 15 minutes.

5. Serve with lettuce spears.

On-the-Fly Mexican-Style Crudo

THIS MEXICAN-STYLE ceviche utilizes a light agua de ají, or "chile water," as a curing agent. With bright lime, numbing jalapeño, and sweet-meets-citrusy orange, it's a delicious, quick, and refreshing snack or light lunch on a hot day. The delicate orange suprêmes beautifully complement the rich and buttery fresh fish.

AGUA DE AJÍ

1 **poblano pepper,** seeded and chopped

3 **celery leaves**

2 **garlic cloves,** peeled and whole

Juice of 6 **limes**

Salt

CRUDO

14 ounces sushi-grade **skinless salmon,** cubed

10 ounces sushi-grade **tuna,** cubed

2 **vine tomatoes,** halved and sliced

2 **oranges,** cut into suprêmes), with juice

6 **green olives,** chopped

½ medium **red onion,** sliced

1 tablespoon drained **capers,** chopped

Salt

Tortilla chips, for serving

TO MAKE THE AGUA DE AJÍ

1. In a blender, combine the poblano pepper, celery leaves, garlic, lime juice, and a pinch of salt and blend until almost smooth. Add a splash of water if necessary to help the ingredients come together.

MAKE THE CRUDO

2. In a nonreactive medium bowl, combine the salmon, tuna, tomatoes, orange suprêmes, a splash of orange juice, olives, red onion, and capers. Pour the agua de ají over everything and toss to combine. Adjust the seasoning with salt to taste.

3. Allow the fish to cure in your refrigerator for at least 20 minutes (a few hours is optimal).

4. Serve with tortilla chips.

Savory Seafood

Fried Black Sea Bass
with Lime & Oregano Buttermilk

THIS RECIPE was adapted from the citrus-marinated fried fish found along the coast of the Dominican Republic. The fish gets a quick marinade, bathing in a zippy lime, oregano, and garlic dressing before being double-coated in seasoned flour and tangy, rich buttermilk. While dishes like the UK's fish and chips need a lot of tartar sauce and citrus to balance the heaviness of the fry, the lime marinade gives this fried sea bass the flavor to stand on its own—though tartar is always a welcome addition, so I threw in a quick tartar sauce on the side as well. While I love how the mildly sweet flavor of the black sea bass complements the bright marinade, red snapper or any white, flaky fish would be delicious in its place.

4 **black sea bass fillets,** rinsed and patted dry

½ teaspoon **dried oregano**

2 teaspoons minced **garlic**

Juice of 2 **limes**

Salt and **freshly ground black pepper**

1 cup **all-purpose flour**

1 teaspoon **garlic powder**

1 teaspoon **onion powder**

½ teaspoon **paprika**

1 cup **buttermilk**

Neutral oil, for frying

2 tablespoons **sweet pickle relish**

¼ cup **mayo**

1 **lime,** sliced into wedges

1. In a nonreactive container, sprinkle the fish with the oregano, garlic, lime juice, 2 teaspoons salt, and ¼ teaspoon pepper. Let marinate for 15 minutes.

2. In a shallow dish, mix the flour with the garlic powder, onion powder, paprika, 1 teaspoon salt, and ½ teaspoon pepper.

3. Pour the buttermilk over the fish. Pull the fish out of the marinade, one piece at a time, allowing any excess liquid to drip off, and dredge in the flour mixture. Shake off any excess flour and dip again in the buttermilk, then dredge again in the flour mixture to double-coat.

4. Pour enough oil into a deep pan to fill it halfway and heat over medium heat to about 350°F.

5. Carefully add the fish in batches and fry on both sides until golden brown, about 6 minutes.

6. In a small bowl, combine the relish and mayo to make a tartar sauce.

7. Serve the fried fish with the tartar sauce and lime wedges on the side.

Broiled Cod
with Parmigiano Crust &
Lemon-Garlic Butter Sauce

THERE'S A SAYING in Portugal that goes, "There are one thousand and one ways to make cod," stemming from Portugal's rich history of worship for the flaky fish. Cod is considered a delicacy in Portugal, and cod recipes have been passed down for centuries. It's a huge part of the culture: The smell of dried, salted cod sparks fond memories of lazy strolls through Portuguese markets.

Of all the ways to cook cod, this is one of my favorites for its ability to achieve so many interesting textures and savory flavors with just 10 minutes of preparation. It's broiled, topped with a Parmesan-panko crust, and broiled once more, becoming deliciously tender and crunchy at the same time. A simple lemon, garlic, and butter sauce brings balance. This is Mediterranean comfort food at its best!

FISH

½ cup grated **Parmesan cheese**

½ cup **panko bread crumbs**

4 tablespoons **unsalted butter**, at room temperature

1 teaspoon **Dijon mustard**

4 **Kalamata olives**, pitted and chopped

¼ teaspoon chopped **fresh rosemary**

TO COOK THE FISH

1. Preheat the broiler to high.

2. In a small bowl, combine the Parmesan, panko, butter, mustard, olives, rosemary, ½ teaspoon salt, and ⅛ teaspoon black pepper. Set the breading mixture aside.

3. Season the cod with the lemon juice and salt and black pepper to taste. Drizzle with enough olive oil to coat. Lay the fish on a sheet pan and broil until cooked through, 3 to 4 minutes.

Salt and **freshly
ground black pepper**

1½ pounds skinless
cod, cut into 4 pieces

Juice of 1 **lemon**

**Extra-virgin olive
oil,** for drizzling

SAUCE

1 tablespoon
extra-virgin olive oil

1 teaspoon minced **garlic**

Pinch of **red chile flakes**

2 tablespoons
fresh lemon juice

1 stick (4 ounces) cold
unsalted butter,
cut into pieces

Salt

MEANWHILE, MAKE THE SAUCE

4. In a small skillet, heat the olive oil over medium-low heat. Add the garlic and sauté until browned. Add the chile flakes and lemon juice and bring to a simmer. Gradually add the cold butter and emulsify until all the butter has been incorporated. Season with salt to taste and set aside.

5. Remove the fish from the broiler and mound the breading mixture on top to make a crust. Broil for 1 minute.

6. Transfer the fish to a large serving platter, drizzle with the sauce, and serve.

Nobu Rip-Off Brown Sugar Miso Cod

MIRIN is often confused with rice vinegar, but their flavor profiles are quite distinct. While both are staples of Japanese cooking, rice vinegar is salty and acidic, while mirin imparts a sweet flavor, more like a Marsala wine. All due credit goes to Nobu for creating a miso cod recipe so simply perfect I wouldn't dare to mess with it. Cod is marinated in a mixture of mirin, honey, brown sugar, and miso until decadently sweet, savory, and delicious. Serve on its own or with steamed broccoli and cooked rice.

½ cup **mirin**

½ cup **miso paste**

½ cup **honey**

¼ cup packed **light brown sugar**

Salt

2 pounds **black cod** or skinless Atlantic cod, cut into 4 portions

1. In a medium bowl, whisk together the mirin, miso, honey, brown sugar, and 1 teaspoon salt. Arrange the cod in a single layer in a broilerproof baking dish and pour the miso mixture over the fish. Allow to marinate for at least 20 minutes (overnight in the fridge would be optimal).

2. Preheat the broiler to low.

3. Place the baking dish with the fish and marinade under the broiler for 8 to 10 minutes.

4. Serve immediately.

Cod
with Olive & Spicy Pepper Sauce

ORIGINATING in the Maghreb in Northwest Africa, harissa is a roasted red pepper and chile paste flavored with garlic, olive oil, citrus, and spices. Traditionally harissa was made by crushing the peppers by hand; the name comes from the Arabic *harasa,* meaning "to break into pieces." This simple weeknight dinner is ever so slightly sweet, tangy, and spicy, with a nicely subtle smokiness. All the flavors found in harissa complement without overpowering each other, making it an ideal condiment for a wide variety of dishes. Skin-on cod gives a slightly richer flavor and more interesting texture to the final dish, but skinless works well, too. Serve with steamed rice or a green salad.

Extra-virgin olive oil, as needed

1 medium **yellow onion,** thickly sliced

3 tablespoons **harissa**

1½ pounds **skin-on cod,** cut into 4 portions

Salt

¼ cup **water**

6 **olives,** halved and pitted

¼ cup chopped **fresh cilantro**

Juice of ½ **lemon**

1. In a small pot, heat 2 tablespoons olive oil over medium-high heat. Once hot, add the onion and sauté for 2 minutes. Pour in the harissa and bring to a simmer.

2. Meanwhile, in a separate sauté pan, add enough olive oil to coat the bottom of the pan and heat over high heat. When the oil shimmers, season the cod on both sides with salt and place in the pan, skin-side down.

3. Sear for 2 minutes on each side, then pour the harissa mixture over the top. Add the water, olives, cilantro, and lemon juice. Cover and simmer for 2 minutes.

4. Drizzle the fish with another tablespoon of olive oil. Taste and adjust the seasoning with more salt, then serve.

Salmon
in Aromatic Coconut Milk

WHILE LEMONGRASS, with its distinct lemon oil aroma, is the most obvious component in terms of flavor in this dish, the evaporated milk is the secret sauce. The shelf-stable product, made by removing most of the water from fresh milk, is well-known for its ability to make your hotel lobby coffee more palatable, but it can also give body to smoothies, oatmeal, soups, and sauces. Here it gives the intensely flavorful broth a delightful velvety texture. Creamy, citrusy, and rich without being too heavy, you may find yourself fighting over who gets the last spoonful to drizzle over their bowl of steaming rice. What's best is that this recipe is just as versatile as it is flavorful. Feel free to substitute whichever white fish is freshest at your local market for the salmon. Delicious on its own, this dish is even better served with steamed white rice for soaking up all the flavor.

1½ pounds **skinless salmon,** cut into large pieces

½ teaspoon **dried oregano**

2 teaspoons **minced garlic,** plus 1 **garlic clove,** peeled and whole

Juice of 2 **limes**

Salt and **freshly ground black pepper**

1 (14-ounce) can **coconut milk**

3 tablespoons **evaporated milk**

1 **lemongrass stalk,** cut into 1-inch pieces

1. In a large bowl, combine the salmon, oregano, minced garlic, lime juice, and salt and pepper to taste. Set aside.

2. In a small pot, combine the coconut milk, evaporated milk, lemongrass, shallot, whole garlic clove, bouillon powder, and a pinch of salt. Bring to a simmer over medium heat. Then set aside.

1 **shallot,** chopped

1 teaspoon **chicken bouillon powder**

Neutral oil, for frying

1 cup **all-purpose flour**

1 medium **yellow onion,** cubed

1 **red bell pepper,** cut into large squares

8 sprigs **cilantro,** for garnish

1 **lime,** cut into wedges, for squeezing

3. Pour ¼ inch of oil into a deep pot and heat over medium heat to 350°F. Line a large plate with paper towels.

4. Place the flour in a shallow dish and dredge the salmon in the flour. Carefully drop the fish pieces into the oil, one by one. Fry until golden brown on each side, about 2 minutes. Use a slotted spoon to transfer the fish to the paper towels to drain.

5. In a sauté pan, heat 2 tablespoons oil over medium-high heat. When the oil is hot, add the onion and bell pepper and cook for 3 minutes. Strain the infused milk into the sauté pan. Add the fish and simmer for 2 minutes.

6. Serve garnished with the cilantro sprigs and lime wedges for squeezing.

Deep-Fried Lobster
with Pepper Jelly

BACK WHEN EUROPEANS first settled in North America, lobsters were so abundant, they would pile up like litter all along the seashore. Considered a "poor man's protein," the crustaceans were fed to prisoners, servants, and anyone who couldn't afford the land animals that were in vogue at the time.

Lobster has since really turned its reputation around, and for good reason: The sweet, succulent meat, when cooked properly, is absolutely delicious. Today, there's something so celebratory and festive about serving lobster. It's one of those showstopping single ingredients where you can see the twinkle in your guests' eyes as soon as you bring it to the table. Here it's seasoned, quickly fried, and served with a stewed sweet pepper jelly. Serve on special occasions when you really want to stun your guests, perhaps with Champagne.

PEPPER JELLY

3 pounds **baby peppers**

Extra-virgin olive oil

3 ounces **sun-dried tomatoes** packed in oil, drained and minced

3 **garlic cloves**, minced

1 tablespoon **honey**

¼ cup **red wine vinegar**

1 tablespoon chopped **fresh rosemary**

TO MAKE THE PEPPER JELLY

1. Stem and seed the baby peppers and slice into rings.

2. In a deep sauté pan, add enough olive oil to cover the bottom of the pan and heat over medium-high heat. Add the sun-dried tomatoes and garlic and cook, stirring, for 1 minute. Add the baby peppers and blister until softened, about 7 minutes. Stir in the honey, vinegar, and rosemary. Set aside.

-recipe & ingredients continue-

LOBSTER

1 cup
all-purpose flour

⅓ cup **cornstarch**

1 tablespoon
fennel pollen

1 tablespoon
Old Bay seasoning

1 tablespoon
garlic powder

1 tablespoon
onion powder

1 tablespoon **ground
white pepper**

2 tablespoons **salt**

3 to 4 quarts **neutral
oil**, for deep-frying

2 **lobsters**
(about 2 pounds each)

TO PREPARE THE LOBSTER

3. In a large bowl, combine the flour, cornstarch, fennel pollen, Old Bay, garlic powder, onion powder, white pepper, and salt.

4. Pour 2 inches of oil into a large deep pot (like a Dutch oven or braiser) and heat over high heat to 375°F.

5. Cut the lobsters in half lengthwise from head to tail, then dredge in the flour mixture.

6. Line a sheet pan with a wire rack. Shake off any excess flour and fry the lobster in batches, cut-side down, for 4 minutes. Flip and fry for 2 to 3 minutes more. Transfer to the wire rack to rest for 2 to 3 minutes.

7. Arrange the lobsters on a platter and top with the pepper jelly.

Crab Cakes *with*
Serrano Pepper Tartar Sauce

CRAB is typically reserved for special occasions or eating out at a restaurant. The truth is, cooking crab at home is simple and quick, especially with lump crabmeat being so easy to buy and use with little preparation necessary, so there is no reason you can't make this dish on a weeknight. This classic crab cake with a serrano tartar sauce comes together in just a few minutes and brings a sense of nostalgia with a slightly spicy surprise.

CRAB CAKES

1 pound **lump crabmeat**

½ cup chopped **fresh parsley**

½ cup chopped **fresh dill**

Grated zest of 1 **lemon**

¼ cup **mayo**

2 tablespoons **Worcestershire sauce**

2 teaspoons **Dijon mustard**

1 teaspoon **seafood seasoning**

¼ teaspoon **Tabasco sauce**

1. Preheat the oven to 350°F.

TO MAKE THE CRAB CAKES

2. In a bowl, combine the crabmeat, parsley, dill, lemon zest, mayo, Worcestershire, mustard, seafood seasoning, Tabasco sauce, and eggs. Form into 4 patties.

3. Place the panko in a shallow dish. Coat the patties in the panko, then transfer to the refrigerator to chill for 10 minutes.

4. In a cast-iron skillet, heat enough olive oil to coat the bottom of the pan over medium heat. Add the crab cakes and sear on one side until golden brown, 2 to 3 minutes. Flip and slide the pan into the oven. Bake for 10 minutes.

-recipe & ingredients continue-

2 large **eggs**, beaten

1 cup **panko bread crumbs**

Extra-virgin olive oil, as needed

QUICK TARTAR SAUCE

2 tablespoons **sweet pickle relish**

¼ cup **mayo**

½ **serrano chile,** minced

Lemon wedges, for serving

MEANWHILE, MAKE THE QUICK TARTAR SAUCE

5. In small bowl, combine the relish, mayo, and chile.

6. Serve the baked crab cakes with the tartar sauce and lemon wedges on the side.

Pu Pu–Style Fried Shrimp
with Pineapple Salsa

I HAD a paper route growing up to earn extra money. As soon as I'd make 50 cents, I'd run to the fishmonger, who would let me buy a single shrimp. I'd buy one, then run home, fry it until crispy, and eat it standing up. It was the ultimate luxury. This dish, with a few added ingredients since those early days, brings back that feeling of biting into that hard-earned indulgence.

All credit goes to the Thai basil's sneakily strong role in flavoring this vibrant appetizer. Sure, the bright and juicy fresh pineapple screams for your attention, but the Thai basil sits back and patiently waits as you start to recognize its unique anise flavor. Unlike its sweeter cousin (sweet basil, the variety that's standard at most American grocery stores), Thai basil can withstand high heat. Serving the basil both fresh and fried, this dish plays on the senses with tons of bold flavors and textures. If you have cornstarch on hand, feel free to use it in place of the potato starch.

PINEAPPLE SALSA

½ **pineapple,** cored and finely diced

2 fresh **Thai green chiles,** minced

12 **Thai basil leaves,** slivered

Juice of 2 **limes**

¼ cup **honey**

2 teaspoons **sambal oelek**

Salt

TO MAKE THE PINEAPPLE SALSA

1. In a small bowl, combine the pineapple, chiles, basil, lime juice, honey, and sambal. Season with salt and set aside.

-recipe & ingredients continue-

FRIED SHRIMP

Neutral oil, for frying

3 large **eggs**

¾ cup **all-purpose flour**

¾ cup **potato starch**

½ teaspoon **ground fennel seeds**

Salt

½ teaspoon **freshly ground black pepper**

1 pound **shrimp,** peeled and deveined

GARNISH

Handful of **Thai basil leaves**

6 fresh **Thai green chiles**

TO FRY THE SHRIMP

2. Pour 1 inch of oil into a deep pan and heat over high heat to about 350°F. Line a tray with paper towels.

3. Set up a dredging station with two shallow dishes: Beat the eggs in one dish. Combine the flour, potato starch, fennel, 1 teaspoon salt, and the pepper in the second dish.

4. Coat the shrimp in the eggs, then transfer to the flour mix and dredge until completely coated. Dust off any excess flour.

5. Working in batches so as not to crowd the pan, add the shrimp to the hot oil, one by one. Fry until golden brown, about 1 minute per side. Transfer to the paper towels to drain. Sprinkle with a small pinch of salt. Keep the oil hot for the garnishes.

TO MAKE THE GARNISH

6. Fry the Thai basil leaves and Thai chiles for 1 minute.

7. Spread the shrimp on a serving platter and top with the fried basil and chiles. Serve with the pineapple salsa on the side.

Pietro's Shrimp Parmesan

CHICKEN PARMIGIANA, or "chicken Parm," was born in the US thanks to Italian immigrants. Here shrimp is given the same five-star treatment: breaded, fried, layered with red sauce, topped with salty aged Parmesan, and broiled until golden brown. You wouldn't find this in Italy. This recipe comes from Pietro's, a classic red sauce joint I worked at in the '80s and '90s. I took Pietro's for granted until I realized years later that they do the best versions of Italian American classics. Fry the shrimp quickly and they'll stay nice and tender, really giving chicken a run for its money.

1 pound **shrimp, peeled and deveined**

1 cup **marinara sauce**

½ cup **all-purpose flour**

Salt and **freshly ground black pepper**

2 large **eggs**

1 cup **Italian seasoned bread crumbs**

½ cup **extra-virgin olive oil**

½ cup freshly grated **Parmesan cheese**

1. Preheat the broiler to high.

2. Butterfly each shrimp by running the tip of a small knife along the back of the shrimp without cutting all the way through, then fold it open.

3. In a small saucepan, heat the marinara over low heat.

4. Set up a breading station with three shallow dishes: Add the flour to one dish and season with salt and pepper. Beat the eggs in a second dish. Place the seasoned bread crumbs in a third dish.

5. Season the shrimp with salt and pepper, then coat them first in the flour, then in the egg, and lastly in the bread crumbs.

6. In a sauté pan, heat the olive oil over medium heat. Add the shrimp in batches so as not to overcrowd the pan and fry until golden brown, about 1 minute on each side.

7. Arrange the fried shrimp in a baking dish in a single layer and spoon 1 tablespoon of the warmed marinara over each shrimp. Sprinkle with the Parmesan.

8. Broil until the cheese melts, about 1 minute. Serve hot.

Fat-Fried Rice,
Super Stoner-Style

FRYING RICE in bacon fat is my favorite trick for taking rice that's a day past its prime and turning it into a meal worthy of sharing with friends. The dryness of the day-old rice plays a crucial role here: The firmer grains hold their own without turning to mush. If you don't have leftover rice burning a hole in your fridge, spread freshly cooked rice over a sheet pan and leave it to dry in your fridge for a few hours. Or to save yourself time, make this stoner-style with a quart of cooked rice from your local take-out restaurant.

6 slices **bacon**, cut crosswise into strips ½ inch wide

¼ cup minced **shallot**

2 tablespoons minced **fresh ginger**

2 tablespoons minced **garlic**

2 medium **carrots**, diced

2 **celery stalks**, diced

12 ounces **shrimp**, peeled, deveined, and diced

2 tablespoons **unsalted butter**

4 large **eggs,** beaten

4 cups **day-old cooked rice**

2 tablespoons **toasted sesame oil**

¼ cup **soy sauce**

½ cup chopped **fresh cilantro**

¼ cup **pineapple preserves**

1. In a large sauté pan, render the bacon over medium heat, stirring, until it's about to turn brown.

2. Add the shallot, ginger, and garlic and sauté for 1 minute. Add the carrots and celery and sauté until tender, about 3 minutes. Add the shrimp and cook until they turn pink, about 1 minute.

3. Push the contents to one side of the pan. Add the butter and let it melt, then pour in the beaten eggs and scramble and mix with the shrimp and vegetables. Add the rice, sesame oil, and soy sauce and fry for 5 minutes.

4. Finish by folding in the cilantro and pineapple preserves.

Perfect Poultry

Almost Francese Lemon-Caper Chicken

THIS IS my simplified version of chicken francese, a classic Italian American dish of pounded chicken in a lemony pan sauce. Though it comes together quickly, it tastes like you spent all day—making it the perfect back-pocket recipe for when you're short on time but want a dish to impress.

2½ pounds **boneless, skinless chicken breasts**

Salt and **freshly ground black pepper**

2 cups **all-purpose flour**

½ cup **extra-virgin olive oil**

1 cup **chicken stock**

1 tablespoon grated **lemon zest**

6 tablespoons **fresh lemon juice** (from about 2 lemons)

2 tablespoons drained **capers**

3 tablespoons chopped **fresh parsley**

6 tablespoons cold **unsalted butter**

1 pound **pasta**, cooked, for serving

1. Slice the chicken breasts into cutlets and season with salt and pepper. Dredge the chicken in the flour and set aside.

2. In a large sauté pan, heat the olive oil over medium-high heat. Working in batches of 1 or 2 cutlets, shallow-fry the chicken until golden brown, about 3 minutes per side. Set aside and repeat with the remaining cutlets.

3. Add the chicken stock to the same pan and scrape up any browned bits on the bottom of the pan, stirring to incorporate them. Cook over medium-high heat to reduce the stock by almost half, about 10 minutes.

4. Add the lemon zest, lemon juice, and capers. Bring back to a simmer and simmer for 1 to 2 minutes. Remove from the heat and add the chicken, half the parsley, and the cold butter. Stir to emulsify.

5. Serve the chicken and sauce over the pasta and garnish with the remaining parsley.

Better-Than-Store-Bought
Chicken Parmesan

THIS CLASSIC dish is delicious, due in part to what's called the Maillard reaction, a chemical reaction that causes the browning of food during cooking. When food is cooked and browned, an array of chemicals react to create hundreds of flavor compounds easily recognizable in foods we love. Here we take full advantage of the Maillard reaction: The chicken is breaded and browned, then topped with sauce and creamy mozzarella, which is broiled until bubbling and—you guessed it—golden brown. All those layers of browning interact to create a rich, complex flavor that makes chicken Parm such a lasting hit. If you don't have a thermometer, you can test the temperature of the oil by dropping in a pinch of bread crumbs before frying the chicken. If they sizzle quickly, your oil is ready to turn your chicken golden brown and delicious.

Pomodoro sauce (from Spaghetti Pomodoro 365, page 26)

2 cups **all-purpose flour**

4 large **eggs**, beaten

2 cups **Italian seasoned bread crumbs**

¼ cup grated **Parmesan cheese**, plus more for garnish

2½ pounds **boneless, skinless chicken breasts**, cut into thin cutlets

Salt and **freshly ground black pepper**

Neutral oil, for shallow-frying

1 pound **mozzarella cheese**, shredded

1. Make the pomodoro sauce as directed.

2. Preheat the broiler to high.

3. While the sauce is cooking, set up three shallow dishes: Place the flour in one dish and the eggs in a second. In the third bowl, toss together the bread crumbs and Parmesan.

4. Season the chicken with salt and pepper. Coat the chicken first in the flour, then in the eggs, and finally in the bread crumbs.

5. Pour 2 inches of oil into a deep pan and heat over medium heat until it reaches 350°F. Working in batches of 1 or 2 cutlets to avoid crowding the pan, fry the cutlets in the hot oil until golden brown, 2 to 4 minutes per side. As they cook, transfer them to a sheet pan.

6. When all the cutlets are cooked, generously sauce the top of each with the pomodoro sauce. Sprinkle with the mozzarella.

7. Place under the broiler and broil until the cheese melts and turns golden brown. Serve garnished with Parmesan.

From the '80s
Chicken Cordon Bleu

WHEN I WAS in the second grade, my mom started working in the kitchen at a public school. Chicken cordon bleu was trendy at that time, and I honestly credit the frozen roulade my mom brought home with inspiring me to become a chef. Growing up Italian, I thought I knew everything there was to know about food. I took one bite into that melty, crispy roll of cheesy goodness and my world quadrupled in size. I realized I had so much to learn.

Serving a roulade is showy in a festive way and always brings a smile to people's faces. Before plating, I recommend you bring your cordon bleu to the table whole and cut into it in front of your guests to show off all that melty cheese. I'm smiling just thinking about it.

1 (10-ounce) **boneless, skinless chicken breast**

Salt and **freshly ground black pepper**

4 ounces sliced **Swiss cheese**

4 ounces thinly sliced **boiled ham**

1. With the chicken breast flat on the cutting board, slice it open horizontally like you're opening a book (but don't cut all the way through). Cover with plastic wrap and tenderize with a meat mallet until flattened to about ¼ inch thick. Season with salt and pepper on both sides.

2. Layer 3 or 4 slices of Swiss cheese on top of the seasoned chicken. Make a layer of 3 or 4 slices of ham. End with 2 or 3 more slices of Swiss cheese.

3. Roll up the chicken lengthwise to form a log. Wrap tightly in plastic wrap and refrigerate for 30 to 45 minutes.

1 cup **potato starch** or **cornstarch**

2 large **eggs**, beaten

1 cup **Italian seasoned bread crumbs**

Neutral oil, for shallow-frying

3 tablespoons **red wine vinegar**

¼ cup **extra-virgin olive oil**

2 teaspoons **whole-grain mustard**

1 tablespoon chopped **fresh parsley**

4. Preheat the oven to 350°F.

5. Set up a breading station with three shallow dishes: Place the potato starch in the first dish, season with salt and pepper, and stir to combine. In the second dish, add the eggs. Add the bread crumbs to the third dish.

6. Toss and coat the chicken roll first in the starch, then in the egg, and lastly in the bread crumbs. Make sure the ends of the chicken roll are breaded to ensure the cheese stays inside while frying.

7. Pour 2 inches of neutral oil into a deep heavy-bottomed pan and heat over medium heat to 315° to 325°F. Line a sheet tray with a wire rack.

8. Add the chicken roll to the hot oil and shallow-fry until golden brown, making sure to rotate and baste when necessary for an even color on all sides, 2 to 3 minutes per side.

9. Transfer the chicken roll to the pan with the rack and bake until the internal temperature reaches 165°F, 5 to 10 minutes.

10. Remove and set on a dish lined with paper towels. Let rest for 2 to 3 minutes.

11. Meanwhile, in a small bowl, whisk together the vinegar, olive oil, and mustard. Season with salt and pepper and whisk until homogeneous and thick. Allow to rest for 1 minute.

12. Slice the cordon bleu crosswise into medallions and plate. Drizzle with the mustard vinaigrette and garnish with the parsley.

Chicken Tinga Enchiladas
in Adobo Sauce

CHICKEN TINGA is a Mexican dish of Puebloan origin in which chicken is shredded and marinated in a sauce of tomato, chipotle in adobo, and sliced onion. Derived from the word *adobar,* meaning "marinate," adobo sauces are found all around the world. Smoky, spicy, slightly earthy, tangy, and sweet, this complex sauce does all the work for you.

To save time, I use store-bought rotisserie chicken and flour tortillas so there's no need to fry. It's perfect for a Sunday lunch or a weeknight dinner at home.

3 tablespoons **neutral oil**

2 medium **white onions**, sliced

3 **garlic cloves**, sliced

1 (28-ounce) can **whole peeled tomatoes**

3 cups **chicken stock**

¼ cup **chipotle peppers in adobo sauce**

1 teaspoon **dried oregano**

¼ teaspoon **freshly ground black pepper**

2 cups shredded **rotisserie chicken**

8 (6-inch) **flour tortillas**

1 cup shredded **cheddar cheese**

½ cup **salsa verde**

½ cup **sour cream**

1. Preheat the oven to 450°F.

2. In a sauté pan, heat the oil over medium heat until shimmering. Add the onions and sauté until translucent, about 3 minutes. Add the garlic and sauté for 1 minute.

3. Use your hands to crush the tomatoes, then add them to the pan, along with the chicken stock, chipotle peppers in adobo sauce, oregano, and black pepper. Bring to a boil, then reduce the heat to medium and simmer for 5 minutes.

4. Add the shredded chicken and cook for 10 minutes.

5. Set a sieve over a large bowl and spoon the chicken mixture in, reserving both the liquid and the chicken mixture.

6. On a clean work surface, lay out the tortillas. Distribute the chicken among the tortillas. Roll up each around the filling, tucking the seam under. Set seam-side down in a 9 × 13-inch baking dish. Pour the reserved liquid over everything. Sprinkle the cheddar over everything.

7. Bake until the cheese has melted, about 5 minutes.

8. Serve the enchiladas topped with salsa verde and a dollop of sour cream.

Chicken Rollatini
with Sage Brown Butter

A VARIATION on the classic Chicken Cordon Bleu (page 164), this dish uses the same fun technique but with a few interesting tweaks: The ham is swapped out for thinly sliced, salty prosciutto, balanced by mild and creamy mozzarella. The predominant flavor in this rollatini comes, surprisingly, from the sauce, a simple and versatile brown butter and sage sauce that adds a more complex richness to this dish. It's also perfect for making a super-quick pasta sauce at home when you only have 10 minutes, so keep it in mind for future recipes.

Browning butter is a culinary technique that takes some practice but is well worth the effort. As the butter melts and foams, the water evaporates and the milk solids begin to toast. There's a fine line between perfectly toasty, caramelized milk solids and burned butter. Use your nose as well as your eyes! When the butter smells toasty and you see brown specks at the bottom, it's ready to be taken off the heat (it will continue to brown as it cools). My tip: Use a light-colored pan and a silicone spatula, and mix constantly.

2 **boneless, skinless chicken breasts**

Salt and **freshly ground black pepper**

4 slices **prosciutto**

4 slices **fresh mozzarella cheese**

1. Preheat the oven to 350°F.

2. With a chicken breast flat on the cutting board, slice it horizontally like you're opening a book (but don't cut all the way through). Lay a piece of plastic wrap over the chicken. Using a meat mallet, pound the chicken out to about ¼ inch thick. Season with salt and pepper on both sides. Repeat with the second chicken breast.

3. Lay 1 slice of prosciutto on each piece of chicken. Follow with 2 slices of mozzarella per piece of chicken and top each with another slice of prosciutto. Roll up the chicken lengthwise to enclose the filling. Wrap tightly in plastic wrap and set in your refrigerator to chill while you get your breading station set up.

-recipe & ingredients continue-

½ cup **all-purpose flour**

2 large **eggs,** beaten

1 cup **seasoned bread crumbs**

¼ cup **extra-virgin olive oil**

5 tablespoons **unsalted butter**

4 **sage leaves**

4. Meanwhile, set up a breading station with three shallow dishes: In the first dish, place the flour. Place the egg in the second dish. Place the bread crumbs in the third dish.

5. Dredge the chicken rollatini in the flour, being careful to keep the roll intact. Roll in the egg, then dredge in the bread crumbs.

6. In a sauté pan, heat the olive oil over medium heat. When the oil is hot, add the chicken and fry until golden brown on all sides, basting with the hot oil to get an even color, about 10 minutes.

7. In small sauté pan, melt the butter over medium heat. Allow the butter to brown, then scatter the sage over the hot butter. Let the sage fry for 1 minute, then season with salt and remove from the heat.

8. To serve, slice the chicken rolls crosswise into medallions. Arrange on a platter and spoon the sage butter over the top.

Extra-Large Chicken & Mushroom Sauté

THIS IS a quick and easy take on another Italian American classic: chicken Marsala. The key to this dish is the deep, rich flavor that comes from cooking the chicken with earthy cremini mushrooms. When stewed in Marsala wine—a fortified wine from Sicily with notes of hazelnut, sweet honey, and vanilla—the mushrooms act like little sponges, soaking up all that sweet and savory flavor. Served over a bowl of hot pasta, this dish is a sure crowd-pleaser (and has been since the early nineteenth century!).

2½ pounds **boneless, skinless chicken breasts**

Salt and freshly **ground black pepper**

2 cups **all-purpose flour**

3 tablespoons **extra-virgin olive oil**

1 pound **cremini mushrooms**, sliced

2 medium **yellow onions**, sliced

½ cup **Marsala wine**

1½ cups **chicken stock**

6 **thyme sprigs**

3 tablespoons **unsalted butter**

1 pound **pasta**, cooked, for serving

1. Season the chicken with salt and pepper. Dredge in the flour.

2. In a sauté pan, heat 2 tablespoons of the olive oil over medium heat. When the oil is hot, sear the chicken on both sides until browned, 5 to 8 minutes per side. Remove and set aside.

3. Add the remaining 1 tablespoon olive oil to the pan. Add the mushrooms and season with salt and pepper. Cook the mushrooms until browned, about 5 minutes. Add the onions and sauté for 1 minute.

4. Pour in the wine and cook over medium-high heat to reduce by half. Add the stock and thyme and cook to reduce by half once more. Stir in the butter and adjust the seasoning with salt and pepper.

5. Return the chicken to the pan, cover, and cook over medium-low heat until the chicken is cooked through and an instant-read thermometer reads 165°F, about 10 minutes.

6. Serve over the pasta.

Serves 4
Total Time: **30 minutes**
Ease of Preparation: **Easy**

Italian American Chunky Lemon Chicken

ORIGINATING in the Eastern Mediterranean, variations of lemon chicken can be found all around the world. I adapted this recipe from the Italian dish pollo al limone. The lemon juice not only provides flavor and acidity but also helps tenderize the chicken, an especially welcome technique for leaner cuts like the breast. Sweet and flavorful spring onions make a bed for the chicken as it roasts, which returns the favor by seasoning the onions with all its drippings. The chiles provide a very subtle hint of spice, but you can always swap them out for sweet red bell pepper if spice isn't your thing. Bursts of tart lemon suprêmes, divorced from their bitter coats, finish the dish, along with butter and fresh parsley. The result is super flavorful, vibrant, juicy, and tender chicken and vegetables bathing in a savory, tart, and velvety sauce.

Extra-virgin olive oil, as needed

2 **garlic cloves**, sliced

2 **fresh long red chiles**, sliced in half lengthwise

4 **spring onions**, white parts halved, green parts cut into 1-inch lengths

Salt and **freshly ground black pepper**

1. Preheat the broiler to low.

2. In a sauté pan, heat 2 tablespoons olive oil over medium heat. When the oil is hot, add the garlic slices and cook until browned, about 3 minutes. Add the chiles and spring onions and sauté until the vegetables are slightly tender but still have a bite, about 3 minutes. Season with salt and pepper.

-recipe & ingredients continue-

2 (14.5-ounce) cans
chicken stock

1 **rosemary sprig**

1 (3- to 5-pound)
whole chicken, cut
into 8 serving pieces

3 large **lemons**

2 tablespoons chopped
fresh flat-leaf parsley

2 tablespoons **unsalted
butter,** sliced into pats

3. Pour in the stock, add the rosemary sprig, and transfer to a baking dish large enough to hold the chicken pieces in one single layer.

4. Season the chicken pieces on all sides with salt and pepper. Arrange the chicken on top of the onion and chile mixture. Drizzle with olive oil, place under the broiler, and broil for 25 minutes, turning every so often so that the pieces don't burn.

5. Meanwhile, cut the lemons into suprêmes: Slice off the tops and bottoms of the lemons so they sit level on your cutting board. Use a paring knife to remove the peel and pith by following the curve of the fruit. Working over a bowl to capture the juices, place the lemon in the palm of your hand and work the paring knife in between the membranes to get the individual segments out; these are the suprêmes. Add the suprêmes to the bowl with their juice, then squeeze the remaining juice from the membranes into the bowl. Stir in the parsley.

6. After the chicken has been under the broiler for 25 minutes, pour the lemon and parsley mixture over the chicken. Distribute the pats of butter all around the chicken and broil for another 5 minutes. Serve hot.

Peru for You Chicken
with Creamy Green Sauce

DEVELOPED in the 1950s by Swiss immigrants to Peru, pollo a la brasa is known for its flavorful meat and crispy skin, a result of a limey marinade packed with aromatic spices. Originally reserved for high-end restaurants in the region, this dish has become popular throughout the country. While the chicken speaks for itself, you may find yourself distracted by the green sauce: It's unbelievably perfect on just about anything. In fact, you should bookmark this page for the green sauce alone—keep it for dipping raw vegetables, put it on your tacos, or serve it with your morning eggs.

MARINATED CHICKEN

5 **garlic cloves,** peeled and whole

1 (½-inch) piece **fresh ginger,** peeled and sliced

Grated zest and juice of 1 **lime**

⅓ cup **soy sauce**

1 tablespoon **extra-virgin olive oil**

1 teaspoon **sugar**

2 teaspoons **ground cumin**

1 teaspoon **smoked paprika**

½ teaspoon **dried oregano**

1 teaspoon **salt**

½ teaspoon **freshly ground black pepper**

4 **boneless, skinless chicken breasts**

TO MARINATE THE CHICKEN

1. In a blender, combine the garlic, ginger, lime zest, lime juice, soy sauce, olive oil, sugar, cumin, smoked paprika, oregano, salt, and black pepper and blend on high until smooth.

2. Pour the marinade over the chicken and refrigerate for at least 30 minutes, or ideally overnight.

3. When ready to cook, preheat the oven to 350°F. Also, heat an outdoor grill to medium or heat a grill pan over medium heat.

4. Pull the chicken from the marinade and grill for 3 minutes on each side. Transfer to a baking dish and bake until the internal temperature reaches 165°F, 10 to 15 minutes.

-recipe & ingredients continue-

GREEN SAUCE

1 cup chopped **cilantro leaves and tender stems**

2 **scallions,** cut into 1-inch pieces

2 **garlic cloves,** peeled and whole

1 **jalapeño,** sliced

1 **peperoncini**

½ cup **mayo**

¼ cup **whole-milk Greek yogurt**

2 tablespoons crumbled **Cotija cheese**

2 tablespoons **extra-virgin olive oil**

1 tablespoon **fresh lime juice**

½ teaspoon **salt**

¼ teaspoon **freshly ground black pepper**

Cooked rice or **steamed vegetables,** for serving

MEANWHILE, MAKE THE GREEN SAUCE

5. In a blender, combine the cilantro, scallions, garlic, jalapeño, peperoncini, mayo, yogurt, Cotija, olive oil, lime juice, salt, and black pepper and pulse until it's a semismooth consistency.

6. When the chicken is cooked, allow to rest on a cutting board for 1 minute before slicing.

7. Serve with rice or steamed vegetables and the green sauce on the side.

Quick & Easy
Chicken & Provolone Cutlets

KNOWN AS the king of cheese, Parmigiano-Reggiano is traditionally made using only milk from grass-fed cows. The milk is heated before rennet is added, which coagulates the proteins and forms curds. The whey is drained off and salt is added to the curds to enhance the flavor. Not surprisingly, the Italians have strict regulations for what can call itself "Parmigiano-Reggiano": The cheese must come from only certain parts of Italy, can only have select, preapproved ingredients, and must be aged for 1 to 3 years.

While the pregrated Parmesan you can buy in tubs at the supermarket is handy, it pales in comparison to the real deal in terms of flavor, richness, and quality. I'm all for making things quicker and easier whenever possible, but in this case I insist on using authentic Parmigiano-Reggiano and grating it fresh. It is one of the few times in this book where I'll make a case for taking the extra step! Here chicken is wrapped in buttery provolone, given a double crust of cornmeal and Parmigiano-Reggiano, and fried until melty and delicious.

Salt

1½ cups **fine cornmeal**

1 cup freshly grated **Parmigiano-Reggiano cheese**

3 large **eggs,** beaten

2 **boneless, skinless chicken breasts**

Freshly ground black pepper

1. Bring a large pot of generously salted water to a boil.

2. Set up a dredging station with three shallow dishes: Add ¾ cup of the cornmeal to one dish. In a second dish, mix the remaining ¾ cup cornmeal with the Parmigiano. Add the eggs to the third dish.

3. With a chicken breast flat on the cutting board, cut into the fat side of the chicken and slice the breast in half horizontally to make 2 cutlets. Season the cutlets with salt and pepper.

4 slices **provolone cheese**

8 ounces **penne pasta**

¾ cup **neutral oil**

4 tablespoons **unsalted butter**

2 tablespoons **extra-virgin olive oil**

3 **garlic cloves,** thinly sliced

Pinch of **red chile flakes**

1 bunch **broccoli rabe,** cut into 1-inch pieces

2 tablespoons **water**

4. Arrange 1 slice of provolone on top of each cutlet and press the cheese firmly onto the surface. Dredge the chicken and provolone in the plain cornmeal, then dip in the egg to coat, then dredge in the cornmeal/Parmegiano mixture.

5. Add the pasta to the boiling water and cook to al dente according to the package directions. Drain and set aside.

6. Meanwhile, in a sauté pan, heat the neutral oil over medium heat. When the oil is hot, add the chicken, cheese-side down, and fry until the cheese is melted and the chicken is cooked through and golden brown on both sides, about 5 minutes per side.

7. While the chicken is cooking, in a separate sauté pan, melt 2 tablespoons of the butter in the olive oil over medium heat. When the butter has melted, add the garlic and cook until browned, about 2 minutes. Add the chile flakes and broccoli rabe and sauté for 1 minute. Season with salt, add the water, cover, and cook for 3 minutes.

8. Add the remaining 2 tablespoons butter and the cooked pasta to the broccoli rabe. Stir to combine.

9. Divide the pasta among four plates. Top with the chicken cutlets and serve.

Latchkey-Simple
Chicken Curry

"CURRY" is a blanket term for any spiced meat, fish, or vegetable stew that can be found in cuisines around the globe, from the distinctly British curry tikka masala to goat curry in Jamaica.

Today, just about every country has its own version of curry. "Versatile" is an understatement, as this dish can be as simple or as complex as you want to make it. In this version, I combine Madras curry powder, a yellow curry blend from the southern Indian city of Madras (modern-day Chennai) that packs a nice heat, with several of my favorite spices and aromatics. Feel free to substitute whatever vegetables you have on hand and serve with cooked rice for a fuller meal. This dish is super quick and easy to make. In fact, I named it after my memories of being a latchkey kid who had to cook for himself after school. It's easy enough for the latchkey kids.

2 **chicken legs,** cut in half

Salt and **freshly ground black pepper**

½ cup **all-purpose flour**

2 tablespoons **neutral oil**

1. Season the chicken on both sides with salt and pepper. Place the flour into a shallow dish and dredge the chicken in the flour.

2. In a deep sauté pan, heat the oil over medium heat. Add the chicken and cook until golden brown on both sides, 5 to 8 minutes per side. Remove the chicken and set aside.

3. Pour the oil out of the pan and wipe the pan clean with a paper towel.

2 tablespoons **ghee**

1 (½-inch) piece
fresh ginger, peeled
and minced

1 **shallot,** minced

1 tablespoon
minced **garlic**

1 teaspoon **Madras
curry powder**

½ teaspoon **ground
turmeric**

¼ teaspoon
ground cumin

1 cup **chicken stock**

½ cup canned
coconut milk

1 **russet potato,**
peeled and cubed

1 **fresh long red chile,**
seeded and chopped

1 medium **red
onion,** cubed

1 teaspoon **apple
cider vinegar**

1 teaspoon **sugar**

3 tablespoons
mango chutney

¼ cup **heavy cream**

½ cup chopped
fresh cilantro

4. Add 1 tablespoon of the ghee to the pan, set over medium heat, and allow to melt. Add the ginger, shallot, and garlic and sauté for 1 minute. Add the curry powder, turmeric, and cumin. Let the spices bloom for 30 seconds, then pour in the stock and coconut milk. Stir to combine.

5. Return the chicken to the pan and simmer for 10 minutes. Add the potato, cover, and gently simmer until the potato is fork-tender and the chicken is cooked through, about 10 minutes.

6. Meanwhile, in a separate sauté pan, melt the remaining 1 tablespoon ghee over medium-high heat. Add the chile, onion, vinegar, and sugar, and sauté for 2 minutes. Stir the mixture into the curry.

7. When the potatoes and chicken are done, stir in the mango chutney, cream, and cilantro and serve.

Chicken *with Pomegranate Honey & Harissa Sauce*

SUMAC, which means "red" in Medieval French, Latin, and Syrian, is so named for its vibrant color. The small crimson berries, the fruit of the sumac tree, are dried or roasted before being ground into flakes. While sumac is often compared to lemon zest, it has a flavor of its own that's totally unique: Tart and slightly floral, it makes for a concentrated burst of bright flavor. You'll see it used throughout Middle Eastern and Mediterranean cuisine in everything from salad dressings to dry rubs.

Here tart sumac balances the warming spices of the chicken marinade. A combination of pomegranate juice and honey (for a slightly lighter version of a traditional pomegranate molasses) is drizzled over the crispy chicken, which is served with tangy, spicy harissa yogurt on the side. This is a full-flavored Mediterranean home-cooked meal that's ready in just 30 minutes, and I have no doubt that this page will be stained with sumac-tinged fingerprints in no time.

SPICE-RUBBED CHICKEN

1 teaspoon **ground cinnamon**

1 teaspoon **ground coriander**

1 teaspoon **ground sumac**

1 teaspoon **ground turmeric**

½ teaspoon **ground cardamom**

Salt and **freshly ground black pepper**

TO SPICE THE CHICKEN

1. Preheat oven to 350°F.

2. In a small bowl, combine the cinnamon, coriander, sumac, turmeric, cardamom, salt and pepper to taste, and the olive oil. Rub the chicken with the spice mixture. Place the red onion wedges in a baking dish that will hold the chicken in one layer. Add the chicken and pour the water into the bottom of the dish.

3. Transfer to the oven and bake until the internal temperature reaches 165°F, 5 to 8 minutes.

-recipe & ingredients continue-

3 tablespoons
extra-virgin olive oil

4 **boneless, skinless
chicken breasts**

2 medium **red onions,**
cut into wedges

½ cup **water**

POMEGRANATE HONEY

⅓ cup **honey**

1 cup
pomegranate juice

⅛ teaspoon **salt**

HARISSA YOGURT SAUCE

½ cup **whole-milk
Greek yogurt**

1 tablespoon **rose
harissa powder**

2 tablespoons chopped
fresh cilantro

2 tablespoons
chopped **fresh mint**

⅛ teaspoon **salt**

MEANWHILE, MAKE THE POMEGRANATE HONEY

4. In a saucepan, heat the honey over medium-low heat until it's caramelized, about 3 minutes. Stir in the pomegranate juice and salt and cook until syrupy, about 5 minutes.

MAKE THE HARISSA YOGURT SAUCE

5. In a small bowl, combine the yogurt, harissa powder, cilantro, and mint. Season with the salt.

6. To serve, slice the chicken, scoop up the onions, drizzle with the pomegranate honey, and pass the harissa yogurt sauce on the side.

Almost Heaven
Duck Krapow

A POPULAR STREET FOOD and one of the national dishes of Thailand, krapow is a fast and easily prepared dish whose name and distinctive flavor come from Thai basil. Unlike standard basil, Thai basil is sweeter and more anise-flavored, with a numbing effect similar to Sichuan pepper.

For added richness, I swap out the more traditional ground beef or chicken for duck. And while we're on the subject, don't be afraid to cook duck! I have observed my friends and family balking in fear at the thought of cooking duck at home, but in truth, duck is one of the more forgiving meats on the market. It doesn't carry the same risk of salmonella as chicken, so you can cook it to a lower temperature. And because the entire bird is dark meat, it doesn't dry out as easily. If you've been cooking chicken at home, think of it like you've been training with weights and now you're ready for the big race, especially with the foolproof ground duck used here. With that said if duck's not your thing, ground chicken, turkey, or beef would be delicious in its place.

3 tablespoons **fish sauce**

1 tablespoon **sweet soy sauce**

1 tablespoon **dark soy sauce**

1 tablespoon **chili paste**

2 tablespoons **neutral oil**, plus more for frying

4 **garlic cloves**, minced

1 fresh **Thai green chile**, sliced

1 pound **ground duck**

1. In a small bowl, combine the fish sauce, sweet soy, dark soy, and chili paste and set aside.

2. In a large sauté pan, heat the oil over high heat until shimmering. Add the garlic and Thai chile and cook until the garlic starts to brown. Stir in the duck and cook until it starts to brown, about 2 minutes.

3. Add the fish sauce mixture and cook until the sauce reduces, about 5 minutes.

-recipe & ingredients continue-

4 large **eggs**

1 medium **yellow onion,** diced

1 small **red bell pepper,** thinly sliced

1 cup **Thai basil leaves**

¼ teaspoon **ground white pepper**

Cooked white rice, for serving

4. Meanwhile, in a small sauté pan, add enough oil to coat the pan and heat over medium-high heat. When the oil is hot, fry the eggs individually. Set aside.

5. Add the onion, bell pepper, and Thai basil to the duck mixture and stir until the onions are slightly tender. Finish the krapow with the white pepper.

6. Divide among four plates on a bed of white rice. Top with a fried egg and serve.

Mouth-watering Meats

Triple-8 Beef & Broccoli Stir-Fry

THE DISH we know as beef and broccoli traces its roots to *gai lan chao niu rou,* which translates to "gai lan [aka Chinese broccoli] and fried beef." Gai lan is a leafier varietal of broccoli with longer stems and a slightly more bitter flavor. When gai lan was unavailable in the United States, Chinese immigrants had to make do with what they had, creating the culinary classic known today as beef and broccoli or broccoli beef.

Often only thought of as a take-out dish, beef and broccoli is incredibly easy to make at home, with most of the ingredients likely already waiting in your pantry. I've lived on, and have immense respect for, take-out beef and broccoli, so I've named this recipe after my favorite spots. The thinly sliced beef is tossed in a really flavorful sauce and then cooked quickly over high heat, making it virtually impossible to dry out. Shaoxing wine, with its spicy, caramel flavor, can be found in most grocery stores, but if you absolutely must use a substitute, dry sherry is preferred.

1 pound **flank** or **top sirloin steak,** thinly sliced

2 tablespoons **cornstarch**

¼ teaspoon **baking soda**

⅓ cup plus ¼ cup **soy sauce**

1 teaspoon **toasted sesame oil**

¼ teaspoon **ground white pepper**

1. In a bowl, sprinkle the sliced meat with the cornstarch, baking soda, ⅓ cup of the soy sauce, the sesame oil, white pepper, and 1 tablespoon of the neutral oil and toss to coat.

2. Coat the bottom of a large sauté pan with neutral oil and heat over high heat. Add the steak and sear, undisturbed, on one side for 1 minute. Then stir-fry until the steak is almost cooked. Add the garlic, onion, bell pepper, and chiles and stir-fry until tender, about 2 minutes.

2 tablespoons **neutral vegetable oil,** plus more for stir-frying

5 **garlic cloves,** minced

1 medium **yellow onion,** cut into wedges

1 **red bell pepper,** cut into chunks

2 **red chiles,** sliced

2 heads **broccoli,** cut into florets

1½ cups **water**

3 tablespoons **oyster sauce**

1 tablespoon **Shaoxing wine**

2 teaspoons **freshly ground black pepper**

1 teaspoon **sugar**

1 teaspoon **beef bouillon powder**

3. In a separate pan, heat the remaining 1 tablespoon neutral oil over medium-high heat. Add the broccoli and sear on each side until charred. Pour in ½ cup of the water, cover, and steam for 2 minutes.

4. Meanwhile, in a bowl, mix together the remaining 1 cup water, the oyster sauce, Shaoxing wine, remaining ¼ cup soy sauce, the black pepper, sugar, and bouillon powder.

5. Pour the oyster sauce mixture into the pan with the cooked broccoli and cook for 2 minutes more.

6. Plate the broccoli and beef side by side on a platter and serve.

1. Bring broth to a boil in a large pot. **2.** Add vegetables, noodles, and beef and allow to boil. **3.** Divide mixture among 6 bowls and serve.

1 whole **star anise**

1 teaspoon **salt**

1 teaspoon **beef bouillon powder**

¼ cup **soy sauce**

1 tablespoon **chili crisp**

SHABU-SHABU

2 **scallions,** cut into 1-inch pieces

8 ounces **bok choy** or **tatsoi,** cut into 1-inch pieces

1 cup **sugar snap peas,** ends peeled off

4 ounces **king mushrooms,** sliced

3½ ounces **enoki mushrooms,** trimmed and split into 4 pieces

1 pound **shrimp,** peeled and deveined

1 pound **rib eye steak** or **beef belly,** thinly sliced

4 large **eggs**

Chili oil, for garnish

Hoisin sauce, for serving

Chili crisp, for serving

3. In a small saucepan, bring 4 cups water to a boil. Use a spoon to lower the eggs, one by one, into the boiling water, being careful not to break the shell. Boil for 6 minutes, then drain and pour cold water over the eggs. Once cool, peel and set aside.

4. Strain the broth and discard the solids. Return the broth to the pot and bring back to a boil. Drain the noodles, add them to the boiling broth, and boil for 3 minutes. Add the vegetables and cook for 1 minute.

5. Set out four large soup bowls. Use tongs to pull out the noodles and distribute among the bowls. Arrange the shrimp and beef over the noodles. Ladle the hot broth over the shrimp and beef to cook them.

6. Drop a peeled egg into each bowl and garnish with chili oil. Serve with hoisin and chili crisp on the side.

Mustard-Crusted Beef, Portobello Mushrooms & Sautéed Spinach

TENDERLOIN is a long, oval-shaped cut of beef sourced from just beneath the ribs of the cow, right next to the backbone. It's in the same region where you find fellow prime cuts like the NY strip steak, T-bone, and porterhouse. It's an area of muscle that doesn't work very hard, so the meat stays extra tender.

Due to its thicker size and lean makeup, the challenge with beef tenderloin is to get it cooked to your desired doneness without drying and toughening the meat. Here it's pan-roasted to develop a crust and then quickly finished in the oven until cooked to rare. The meat stays juicy with a buttery texture, perfect alongside rich garlic- and thyme-scented mushrooms and lemony wilted spinach.

-recipe continues-

ROASTED PORTOBELLO MUSHROOMS

2 pounds **portobello mushrooms,** stemmed

2 tablespoons **extra-virgin olive oil**

2 **garlic cloves,** minced

2 teaspoons **fresh thyme**

Sea salt and **freshly ground black pepper**

⅓ cup **red wine vinegar**

¼ cup **ghee,** melted

STEAKS

¼ cup **whole-grain mustard**

1 tablespoon **Dijon mustard**

2 tablespoons **extra-virgin olive oil**

4 (6- to 8-ounce) **beef tenderloin steaks**

Sea salt and **freshly ground black pepper**

Leaves from 1 **rosemary sprig,** chopped

¼ cup chopped **fresh parsley**

1. Preheat the oven to 425°F. Line a baking sheet with foil.

TO ROAST THE PORTOBELLOS

2. In a large bowl, toss together the mushrooms, olive oil, garlic, thyme, and salt and pepper to taste until evenly coated. Spread the mushrooms on the foil-lined baking sheet and roast until golden and tender, 18 to 20 minutes, turning halfway through. Drizzle the vinegar and melted ghee over the mushrooms and toss to coat.

MEANWHILE, COOK THE STEAKS

3. In a small bowl, whisk together the whole-grain and Dijon mustards. Heat a large sauté pan over high heat and add the olive oil. Season both sides of the steaks generously with salt and pepper. Add the steaks to the pan and sear for up to 2 minutes on the first side. Flip and top the steaks with the mustard mixture.

4. Pat the chopped rosemary and parsley evenly over the top of the steaks, transfer to the oven, and cook until the beef reaches your desired doneness. For rare, look for an internal temperature of 125°F.

SPINACH

1½ pounds **baby spinach,** washed and fully dried

2 tablespoons **cornstarch**

1 tablespoon **extra-virgin olive oil**

5 **garlic cloves,** thinly sliced

½ teaspoon **red chile flakes**

Sea salt and **freshly ground black pepper**

½ **lemon**

¼ cup chopped **fresh parsley,** for garnish

MEANWHILE, SAUTÉ THE SPINACH

5. In a bowl, toss the spinach with the cornstarch and set aside.

6. Heat a large sauté pan over high heat. Add the olive oil and garlic and cook until golden brown, about 2 minutes. Add the chile flakes and cook for 30 seconds.

7. Add the spinach to the hot pan and cook until tender, about 3 minutes. Season with salt and black pepper. Squeeze the lemon over the spinach.

8. To serve, garnish the mushrooms with the parsley and top with the steak and spinach on the side.

Serves 4
Total Time: **15 minutes**
Ease of Preparation: **Moderate**

2-Star Sirloin Steak & Fried Eggs

AUSTRALIAN NATIONAL DISH turned American breakfast classic, steak and eggs was first introduced to the US when Marine Corps members were stationed with Australian Allied soldiers during World War II. Today the dish has been immortalized as the "astronaut's breakfast," thanks in part to NASA, which famously served it to Alan Shepard before he became the first American in space in 1961.

For people like myself who haven't ventured off into outer space quite yet, the glorious combination of juicy pan-seared steak and a runny fried egg still holds fond memories. Working in kitchens, I was often off work—and hungry—at odd hours. When I would get off my shift at four o'clock in the morning, there was nothing that hit the spot quite like steak and eggs and a "loaded" Bloody Mary (page 291).

This is my version of that favorite diner order from back in the day, and I must say, it's just as delicious at 4 p.m. as it is at 4 a.m. The eggs are fried and basted in plenty of oil, a technique I love for getting eggs with a crispy edge and runny yolks that never stick to the pan. The steak is pan-seared to medium-rare, and all the juicy, runny goodness is topped with crispy fried shallots. It's perfect for breakfast, lunch, and dinner.

Neutral oil

1 cup thinly sliced **shallots**

½ cup **cornstarch**

Salt

2 (16-ounce) **sirloin steaks**

Cracked black pepper

4 tablespoons **unsalted butter**

4 **thyme sprigs**

2 **garlic cloves,** peeled and whole

4 large **eggs**

Steak sauce, for serving

1. Pour 1 inch of oil into a deep pot and heat over medium-high heat to 350°F. Line a tray with paper towels.

2. In a small bowl, mix the shallots with the cornstarch. When the oil reaches temp, drop the shallots into the oil and stir continuously until the shallots are crisp and about to turn golden brown, about 5 minutes. With a slotted spoon, transfer the shallots to the paper towels to drain. Season with salt.

3. Heat a cast-iron skillet over high heat. Season the steaks with salt and cracked pepper. Add them to the pan, press down lightly to get an even sear, and cook, undisturbed, until the steaks start to release from the pan easily, about 2 minutes.

4. Flip the steaks and add the butter, thyme, and garlic to one side of the pan. Tilt the pan and use a large metal spoon to baste the steaks with the melted aromatic butter for 2 minutes.

5. Use tongs to pick the steaks up and set them on their sides to caramelize the fat cap, about 2 minutes.

6. Transfer the steaks to a cutting board to rest for 1 minute.

7. Meanwhile, in a small sauté pan, heat ¼ cup oil over medium-high heat. Crack an egg into the oil and baste until the whites have cooked, then season with a pinch of salt. Repeat to fry the remaining eggs.

8. Slice the steak and arrange on four plates. Place a fried egg on top of the sliced steak and garnish with the fried shallots. Pass steak sauce on the side.

Nineteenth-Century Steak Diane

NAMED FOR DIANA, the Roman goddess of the hunt, sauce Diane comes together thanks to a simple technique: lighting Cognac on fire. While the display may garner some "oohs" and "aahs" from your guests, it's more than just for show. The flames intensify the sauce's flavor and cook off the alcohol very quickly, leading to a nice caramelization without any off-putting alcohol taste and adding a layer of complexity in mere seconds. Avoid a nonstick pan, make sure the alcohol is warm but not ripping hot, and use a long lighter.

2 tablespoons **extra-virgin olive oil**

4 (14-ounce) **boneless sirloin steaks**

Salt and **freshly ground black pepper**

2 tablespoons **unsalted butter**

¼ cup minced **shallot**

2 teaspoons minced **garlic**

8 ounces **baby bella mushrooms,** sliced

¼ cup **Cognac**

¼ cup **heavy cream**

1 tablespoon **Dijon mustard**

Dash of **Tabasco sauce**

1 tablespoon chopped **fresh rosemary**

1. Heat a cast-iron skillet over medium-high heat and add the olive oil. Generously season the steaks with salt and pepper, add to the hot oil, and sear for 3 minutes on each side.

2. Transfer the steaks to a cutting board to rest.

3. Pour out any excess fat from the pan. Add the butter, shallot, garlic, and mushrooms and sauté for 1 minute.

4. Pour the Cognac into the skillet. Use a long lighter to ignite the alcohol fumes and flambé. When the flames die out, add the cream and simmer to reduce by half.

5. Season with the mustard, Tabasco, and salt and pepper to taste.

6. Slice the steaks, pour the sauce over them, and garnish with the rosemary.

Beef & Lamb Kofta
with Tzatziki Sauce

I WORKED with a chef from North Africa who made these meatballs (kofta) for family meal. I was nervous—I had heard rumblings from the staff about how no one (except me) liked lamb. But by the end of family meal, there was not a single kofta left—the blend of seasonings was so expertly executed and the meat so perfectly cooked that people were lining up for seconds.

This recipe is inspired by that family meal, with juicy, beautifully seasoned meatballs and a classic tzatziki. I love kofta's unique torpedo shape, as it gives more surface area for achieving a crispy golden brown crust. The tart and herby tzatziki is perfect for spooning on the juicy meatballs, but it is also a delicious side dish for serving alongside just about any main, from light salads, dips, and mezzes to grilled meats.

KOFTA

1 pound **ground lamb**

12 ounces **ground beef (70/30)**

½ **red bell pepper,** finely diced

½ **green bell pepper,** finely diced

½ medium **yellow onion,** diced

3 **garlic cloves,** minced

¼ cup chopped **fresh cilantro**

2 teaspoons **paprika**

1½ teaspoons **ras el hanout**

1. Heat a grill pan over medium heat.

TO MAKE THE KOFTA

2. In a medium bowl, mix the lamb, beef, bell peppers, onion, garlic, cilantro, paprika, ras el hanout, cayenne, salt, and black pepper until just combined.

3. Divide the mixture into 8 equal portions. Shape each portion into a log and thread a skewer through the center.

-recipe & ingredients continue-

½ teaspoon **cayenne pepper**

2 teaspoons **salt**

2 teaspoons **freshly ground black pepper**

6 **metal skewers**

TZATZIKI SAUCE

1 cup **whole-milk Greek yogurt**

½ **cucumber,** peeled, seeded, and sliced

2 **garlic cloves,** grated

2 tablespoons chopped **fresh dill**

2 tablespoons **fresh lemon juice**

Pinch of **cayenne pepper**

1 teaspoon **salt**

Freshly ground black pepper

TO MAKE THE TZATZIKI SAUCE

4. In a bowl, combine the yogurt, cucumber, garlic, dill, lemon juice, cayenne, salt, and black pepper to taste.

5. Grill the kofta until the internal temperature reaches 140° to 150°F, about 3 minutes per side.

6. Serve the kofta on a platter with the tzatziki on the side.

First-Draft Fried Pork Chops *in Prune Butter Sauce*

ONE OF the few very plump dried fruits, prune has the flavor of concentrated plum—intensely sweet with a subtle acidity. They're loaded with good minerals, high in iron and fiber, and have no added sugar. Here pork chops are pan-fried and finished in the oven while both dried prunes and prune baby food—a cheeky trick for a low-effort prune puree—are made into a succulent sauce. These First-Draft Fried Pork Chops were so good the first time I didn't touch the recipe. Serve with mashed potatoes or a simple green salad.

4 **prunes**

4 **boneless pork loin chops** (about 4 ounces each)

Salt and **freshly ground black pepper**

¼ cup **all-purpose flour**

¼ cup **potato starch**

¼ cup **neutral oil**

2 (4-ounce) jars **prune baby food**

4 teaspoons **Dijon mustard**

1 teaspoon **sherry vinegar**

4 tablespoons cold **unsalted butter**

1. Preheat the oven to 375°F.

2. Halve the prunes, set in a bowl of warm water, and set aside to soak while you prepare the pork chops.

3. Lay plastic wrap over a pork chop and use a meat mallet to lightly pound it to a 1½-inch thickness. Repeat for all the chops and season them on both sides with salt and pepper.

4. In a shallow dish, mix together the flour and potato starch. Season with salt and pepper. Dredge the pork chops in the flour mixture.

5. Heat an ovenproof sauté pan over medium-high heat. Pour the oil into the pan and when the oil is hot, add the pork chops. Fry for 3 minutes on each side.

6. Slide the pan into the oven and cook until the pork is cooked through, about 10 minutes.

7. Drain the prunes. In a sauté pan, combine the prunes, prune baby food, mustard, and vinegar. Bring to a simmer over medium heat. Stir in the cold butter, 1 tablespoon at a time, until emulsified. Season with salt and pepper.

8. Spoon the sauce over the pork chops and serve.

Super-Delish Pork Schnitzel
with German Potato Salad

SCHNITZEL—a cutlet of meat typically breaded and fried—exists in different forms around the world, from chicken fried steak in the US to tonkatsu in Japan. This recipe is my take on what's arguably the most famous rendition of the fried delight: the Wienerschnitzel, one of Austria's national dishes, which can be found throughout Vienna everywhere from street stalls to fancy restaurants.

In my version, the leanest and most tender cut of pork replaces the more traditional veal. A honey mustard sauce, which takes the place of the usual lemon wedges, pairs nicely with the meat and gives it an interesting layer of sweet and sour flavor. If you have cornstarch on hand, feel free to use it in place of the potato starch. Served alongside schnitzel or on its own, the acidic German potato salad is a sure hit—save the recipe for your next potluck.

GERMAN POTATO SALAD

4 russet potatoes

Salt

6 slices **bacon**, diced

1 medium **red onion**, finely diced

½ cup **white wine vinegar**

½ cup **water**

2 tablespoons **sugar**

2 tablespoons **Dijon mustard**

2 **scallions**, sliced

Freshly ground black pepper

TO MAKE THE GERMAN POTATO SALAD

1. Add the potatoes to a pot and add salted water to cover. Bring to a boil and cook until they're tender but still maintain their shape, about 20 minutes.

2. Meanwhile, in a sauté pan, cook the bacon over medium heat until the fat has rendered and the bacon has begun to caramelize, about 2 minutes. Add the onion and cook until translucent, about 2 minutes. Add the vinegar, water, sugar, and salt to taste. Cook until reduced by half, about 10 minutes.

3. Peel the potatoes while still hot, then thinly shave on the slicing blade of a box grater.

-recipe & ingredients continue-

SCHNITZEL

½ cup
all-purpose flour

½ cup **potato starch**

2 large **eggs,** beaten

1 cup **seasoned bread crumbs**

2 pounds **pork loin**

Salt and **freshly ground black pepper**

½ cup **neutral vegetable oil**

HONEY MUSTARD SAUCE

2 tablespoons **Dijon mustard**

2 teaspoons **whole-grain mustard**

2 tablespoons **honey**

1 teaspoon **fresh lemon juice**

4. Add the sliced potatoes, mustard, and scallions to the pan with the bacon and onions and stir to combine. Season with salt and pepper. Keep warm while you ready the schnitzel.

TO PREPARE THE SCHNITZEL

5. Set up a breading station in three shallow dishes: Combine the flour and potato starch in one dish. Place the eggs in the second dish. Spread the bread crumbs in the third dish.

6. Slice the pork loin into 4 equal pieces. Lay plastic wrap over a slice of pork and lightly pound to a ¼-inch thickness.

7. Season the pork with salt and pepper, then dredge in the flour. Shake off any excess flour and dip into the egg, then finally dredge in the bread crumbs. Set aside.

8. Line a tray with paper towels. In a deep skillet, heat the neutral oil over medium-high heat. When the oil is hot, fry each schnitzel until golden brown on both sides, about 3 minutes per side. Transfer the cooked schnitzel to the paper towels to drain.

TO MAKE THE HONEY MUSTARD SAUCE

9. In a small bowl, combine both mustards, the honey, and the lemon juice.

10. Serve the schnitzel and potato salad with the honey mustard sauce alongside.

Pork Chops *in Bacon Gravy* (*Heart Attack Sold Separately*)

BULL-DOG brand tonkatsu sauce adds a dimension to this simple, quick, and super-rich dish. The Japanese condiment, made by stewing vegetables and fruit and seasoning with vinegar, salt, and spices, is like a thicker version of Worcestershire sauce (not unlike HP or brown sauce in the UK). Thick and sweet Bull-Dog works with the dry vermouth's herbal, warming spice flavor to add complexity to this gravy in just a few minutes' time.

4 slices **bacon,** cut crosswise into strips ½ inch wide

4 **boneless pork loin chops**

Salt and **freshly ground black pepper**

2 **garlic cloves,** thinly sliced

⅔ cup **dry vermouth**

2 cups **chicken stock**

½ teaspoon **chicken bouillon powder**

2 tablespoons **Bull-Dog tonkatsu sauce**

1. Preheat the oven to 375°F.

2. In a large sauté pan, render the bacon over medium-high heat until it starts to brown. Remove from the pan and set aside.

3. Season the pork chops generously with salt and pepper.

4. Add the chops to the bacon fat in the pan and sear on each side for about 2 minutes.

5. Transfer the pork to a baking dish and bake until cooked through, 7 to 10 minutes.

6. Meanwhile, add the garlic to the sauté pan and cook until browned, about 3 minutes. Add the vermouth to deglaze the pan, scraping up the browned bits from the bottom of the pan. Cook until reduced by half.

7. Add the stock and bouillon powder and bring to a boil. Reduce the heat to maintain a simmer and cook until reduced by half, 4 to 6 minutes.

8. Return the bacon to the pan and stir in the Bull-Dog sauce.

9. Serve the pork chops smothered in the bacon gravy.

Pork Chops
in Citrus Mojo Chino Latino

ORIGINALLY from the Canary Islands, the term mojo encompasses several types of sauce centered around local chiles, olive oil, and seasonings. This recipe is inspired by the Cuban style of green mojo, with orange juice being the main flavor base. Traditionally made with sour orange juice, this sauce uses lime to balance the sweetness of the oranges that are more readily available in the US. If you can get your hands on sour oranges, feel free to swap those in instead; just be sure to reduce the amount of lime. Served here with a simple pan-seared pork chop, this mojo recipe also makes a delicious marinade, dip, or coleslaw dressing.

MOJO

Juice of 2 **limes**

Juice of 1 **orange**

½ cup **cilantro sprigs**

¼ **jalapeño**, seeded

3 **garlic cloves,** peeled and whole

⅓ cup **extra-virgin olive oil**

2 teaspoons **sugar**

1 teaspoon **salt**

PORK CHOPS

Extra-virgin olive oil, for cooking

4 (1-inch-thick) **bone-in pork chops**

Salt and **freshly ground black pepper**

1. Preheat the oven to 400°F.

TO MAKE THE MOJO

2. In a blender, combine the lime juice, orange juice, cilantro, jalapeño, garlic, olive oil, sugar, and salt and blend until smooth. Set aside.

TO COOK THE PORK CHOPS

3. Heat a cast-iron skillet or other ovenproof pan over high heat and add 2 tablespoons olive oil. Pat the meat dry with a paper towel, then season generously with salt and black pepper. When the pan is screaming hot, add the pork chops and sear for 3 minutes on one side.

4. Flip the chops, transfer the pan to the oven, and cook until warm in the center, 8 to 10 minutes.

5. Place the chops on a platter, drizzle with the mojo, and serve.

Sunday Suppers

Leisurely Recipes for Gatherings & Special Occasions

Many of the dishes in this chapter take longer than 30 minutes to prepare, but I promise they're well worth the extra time. These are a handful of my favorite recipes, the ones I save for leisurely Sundays, holidays, birthdays, anniversaries, and dinner parties (plus my favorite cocktail recipe for good measure). They're festive and fun and decadent and sure to impress.

—Rocco

Garlic & Horseradish Crusted Rib Roast

with Root Vegetable & Red Wine Gravy

EVERY YEAR, I host my family for the holidays and make these ribs. It's become my tradition, what people know to expect. I imagine if I were to make anything else, chaos would ensue. In fact, whether I like it or not, I get the full rundown at the end of each year on how it compared to the last. This recipe is from my best year. Reviews aside, my family all cozied up at my place eating this rib roast together is my idea of nirvana.

The tradition of prime rib for Christmas dinner started during the Industrial Revolution. Around that time, meat butchering became more commercialized, granting greater access to prime cuts. Today, the tradition lives on, with rib roast serving not only as a beautiful presentation piece, but also the most deliciously juicy and tender cut of beef you can get. Roasted "standing" on its bones, the meat never touches the pan, yielding a buttery, juicy, evenly cooked rib roast every time.

1 (4- to 5-rib) **bone-in dry-aged prime standing rib roast** (10 to 12 pounds)

¼ cup **fine sea salt**

Freshly ground black pepper

CRUST

10 **garlic cloves,** coarsely chopped

1. Preheat the oven to 450°F.

2. Season the roast with the salt and generous amounts of pepper.

TO MAKE THE CRUST

3. In a food processor, combine the garlic, onion, horseradish, oregano, flour, and mayonnaise and pulse to form a rough paste. Spread the paste on the top and sides of the roast.

-recipe & ingredients continue-

1 medium **yellow onion,** chopped

3 tablespoons **prepared horseradish,** drained, plus more for serving

¼ cup **fresh oregano leaves**

3 tablespoons **all-purpose flour**

½ cup **mayonnaise**

ROASTING

2 medium **yellow onions,** cut into large chunks (about 2 cups)

2 large **carrots,** cut into large chunks (about 1 cup)

1 medium **turnip,** peeled and cut into large chunks (about 1 cup)

1 small **celery root,** peeled and cut into large chunks (about 1 cup)

10 **garlic cloves,** peeled and whole

2 cups **chicken stock**

GRAVY

3 slices **bacon,** cut crosswise into strips ¼ inch wide

3 tablespoons **all-purpose flour**

1 cup **dry red wine**

3 cups **chicken stock**

2 **oregano sprigs**

TO SET UP THE ROASTING PAN

4. Place the onions, carrots, turnip, celery root, and garlic in a large roasting pan. Pour the chicken stock over the vegetables.

5. Place the rib roast, crusted-side up and rib-side down, on top of the vegetables. Insert an oven-safe meat thermometer into the thickest part of the roast (called the center of the eye), being careful not to touch the bone.

6. Place the roast in the oven and roast for 15 minutes.

7. Reduce the oven temperature to 250°F and continue to cook until the internal temperature reaches 130°F, about 20 minutes per pound, or 3½ to 4 hours, depending on the size of your roast.

8. Move the roast to a cutting board and cover it loosely with foil. Let it rest for at least 30 minutes before carving.

MEANWHILE, MAKE THE GRAVY

9. Pour all the juices from the pan into a gravy separator.

10. Place the roasting pan with the vegetables on the stovetop over medium-low heat. Add the bacon and cook until the bacon is warm. Stir in the flour and cook for 5 minutes. Pour in the wine, stirring and scraping up any browned bits from the bottom of the pan. Cook and stir until the wine reduces by half.

11. Add the chicken stock, defatted meat juices, and oregano and reduce to a simmer. Simmer for 30 minutes, skimming the fat off the top periodically.

12. Meanwhile, remove the fat layer from the roast and slice the roast using an electric knife.

13. Strain the gravy or serve as is, depending on your preference.

14. Serve the carved roast with the hot gravy and prepared horseradish.

Homemade Citrus-Cured Gravlax

I BET YOU THINK of curing salmon as a magic trick only experienced chefs and old-school deli owners can pull off, but in truth, you can easily do it yourself at home. The secret is quite simple: salt. The basic premise is to cover the fish with enough salt to chemically alter the protein structure and kill any microbial life on the surface, preserving a nice cut of fish to keep on hand for a luxurious breakfast or a wow-worthy appetizer.

In this recipe, you'll learn to cure your own salmon easily at home in one of my favorite styles, gravlax. A Nordic dish—like lox, but with a more delicate flavor—gravlax is traditionally cured underground using both salt and sugar, with spruce twigs added for flavor. If you don't feel like going foraging for spruce twigs and digging a hole in your garden, adding plenty of fresh dill and then weighing down the fish with a couple of dinner plates and a heavy can from your pantry does the job perfectly. The result is a luxurious, lightly cured salmon, which is absolutely beautiful alongside the freshest rye bread you can source; it's just as delicious with crispy bagel chips.

Though this dish takes just a few minutes to prepare, give yourself at least 6 hours for the fish to cure. I like to prepare the salmon on a Friday afternoon and let it do its thing in my refrigerator. I wake up on Saturday morning, make myself an espresso, toast up some rye bread, and start my weekend with a beautiful homemade breakfast spread complete with fresh vegetables.

-recipe continues-

GRAVLAX

¼ cup **fine sea salt**

2 tablespoons **sugar**

Grated zest of 1 **orange**

Grated zest of 1 **lime**

Grated zest of 1 **lemon**

¼ cup chopped **fresh dill**

1 tablespoon **pink peppercorns**, crushed with a mortar and pestle

1½ pounds **skin-on salmon fillet**, pin bones removed

FOR SERVING

1 **English cucumber**, sliced

1 medium **red onion**, sliced

Mixed salad greens

1 **lemon**, cut into wedges

Caper berries

Sliced rye bread, halved, or **crispy bagel chips**

TO MAKE THE GRAVLAX

1. In a small bowl, combine the salt, sugar, citrus zests, dill, and pink peppercorns.

2. Cut the salmon into two even halves and set skin-side down. Divide the citrus/dill/salt mixture between the halves, rubbing the flesh side of each piece of salmon. Flip one half over onto the other piece of salmon, sandwiching the flesh sides together with the skin side facing out.

3. Wrap in parchment paper, then wrap again tightly in plastic wrap. Place on a plate and weight the top with a couple of dinner plates and an unopened can. Refrigerate for 6 to 8 hours.

TO SERVE

4. Unwrap the salmon, rinse under cool water, and pat dry with a paper towel. Use a long, sharp knife to thinly slice the gravlax on a diagonal and assemble on a platter.

5. Serve on a large platter with the sliced cucumber, red onion, salad greens, lemon wedges, caper berries, and rye bread and let your guests serve themselves.

Butterscotch-Glazed Short Ribs of Beef
with Taro & Truffle Mash

WHILE prime short ribs bring this dish to the next level, this recipe is sure to stun your guests with any short ribs from your market. The meat is slowly braised in a wine and Cognac reduction with dates, lemongrass, and ginger, giving an intriguing flavor profile you wouldn't necessarily see at your average steak house. To finish, the ribs are basted with a buttery sweet-tart mixture (called a gastrique) and slowly simmered until they're fall-apart tender and full of meaty, complex flavor.

HERBS AND SPICES

2 **tarragon sprigs**

2 **rosemary sprigs**

4 **thyme sprigs**

4 **juniper berries**

1 teaspoon **mustard seeds**

½ teaspoon **coriander seeds**

2 teaspoons **black peppercorns**

2 **whole cloves**

BRAISED SHORT RIBS

2 **leeks**

6 **dates**, halved and pitted

½ cup **Cognac**

1. Preheat the oven to 325°F.

TO PREP THE HERB BOUQUET AND SPICE BAG

2. Use kitchen twine to tie the tarragon, rosemary, and thyme sprigs together, creating an herb bouquet. Cut out a square of cheesecloth, place the juniper berries, mustard seeds, coriander seeds, peppercorns, and cloves in the middle, and tie closed with kitchen twine. Set the herb bouquet and spice bag aside.

PREPARE THE SHORT RIBS

3. Trim the dark green tops off the leeks and cut the white and pale-green portions crosswise into ¼-inch-wide slices. Add them to a bowl of cold water and swish to clean. Drain, rinse, and set aside.

4. Soak the dates in the Cognac and set aside while you prep the ribs.

-recipe & ingredients continue-

4 pounds **boneless short ribs**, cut into 6 portions

Salt and **freshly ground black pepper**

Neutral oil

10 **garlic cloves**, minced

1 **lemongrass stalk**, lower third only, peeled to the inner stalk and sliced

1 (3-inch) piece **fresh ginger**, peeled and thinly sliced

7 **shallots**, sliced

1½ cups diced **carrots** (about 2)

1 (750ml) bottle **red Bordeaux wine**

6 **tomatoes**, diced (about 3 cups)

2 **celery stalks**, cut into 2-inch lengths

5¼ cups **chicken stock**

5. Season the short ribs with salt and pepper. Heat 1 tablespoon oil in a large Dutch oven over high heat. When the oil smokes, sear the short ribs in batches until golden brown on all sides. Transfer to a plate and set aside.

6. Add the garlic, lemongrass, and ginger to the Dutch oven and sauté until translucent and aromatic, about 3 minutes. Add the shallots and sauté until very soft and almost falling apart, about 6 minutes. Add the leeks and carrots and sauté for 3 minutes more.

7. Add the Cognac and date mixture and stir, scraping up the browned bits from the bottom of the pot. Simmer until the alcohol has evaporated and the pot is almost dry.

8. Pour in the wine and cook until reduced by one-third, about 30 minutes.

9. Add the herb bouquet, spice bag, tomatoes, celery, and chicken stock to the pot. Cover, transfer to the oven, and braise for 1½ hours.

10. While the short ribs are braising, make the taro and truffle mash and keep warm.

11. After 1½ hours, use a cake tester or small paring knife to check for tenderness of the short ribs: If the short rib slips off easily, it's ready, but taste for good measure. Discard the herb and spice bundles. Remove the short ribs from the pot and cover to keep warm. Strain the liquid through a sieve set in a bowl.

-recipe & ingredients continue-

Taro & Truffle Mash
(opposite)

GASTRIQUE

4 tablespoons
unsalted butter

2 medium **yellow onions,**
quartered

1½ cups packed
light brown sugar

1¼ cups **apple
cider vinegar**

Chopped **fresh
parsley,** for garnish

TO MAKE THE GASTRIQUE

12. In a large sauté pan, melt the butter over medium-low heat. Add the onions and sauté for 5 minutes.

13. Add the brown sugar, and once it has melted and begun to caramelize, pour in the vinegar. Allow the vinegar to reduce by half, about 10 minutes. Pour in the braising liquid and reduce until syrupy, about 20 minutes.

14. Add the short ribs to the pan and use a large metal spoon to baste the ribs with the gastrique. Cover the short ribs and simmer for another 20 minutes over low heat.

15. Serve the short ribs over the Taro & Truffle Mash, garnished with parsley.

Taro & Truffle Mash

1 pound **taro root,** peeled and cut into large chunks

1 pound **Japanese sweet potato,** peeled and cut into large chunks

3 tablespoons **truffle butter**

4 tablespoons **unsalted butter**

1 teaspoon minced **fresh chives**

1 teaspoon minced **fresh parsley**

1 teaspoon minced **fresh tarragon**

Salt and **freshly ground black pepper**

1. In a large pot, combine the taro and sweet potato and add water to cover. Bring to a boil and cook until fork-tender, 25 to 30 minutes.

2. Drain and transfer to a large serving bowl. Add the truffle butter and butter and mash just as you would mashed potatoes.

3. Mix in the chives, parsley, and tarragon. Taste and season with salt and pepper.

Mussels & Shrimp Boil
with Cajun Garlic Butter

ENTER the shellfish boil—yet another example of a fun and festive dish to share. Nothing says "party" like gathering with friends outdoors on a hot day with music blasting and piles of shellfish stacked high on newspaper. That's the spirit I'm going for with this dish, which is inspired by Cajun cuisine, a distinctly Louisianan style that combines French, Spanish, and African influences to make something totally unique. Though you can serve the boiled shellfish in piles and with bibs New Orleans–style, I've made things slightly easier—and less messy—here, with bowls and prepeeled shrimp. Bibs or not, the spirit, and flavor, remains just as vibrant.

CAJUN GARLIC BUTTER

Extra-virgin olive oil

6 garlic cloves, minced

2 tablespoons
Cajun seasoning

1 stick (4 ounces)
unsalted butter

TO MAKE THE CAJUN GARLIC BUTTER

1. Pour ½ inch of olive oil into a deep pot and set over medium heat. Once the oil is hot, add the garlic and carefully brown, stirring often and adjusting the heat as necessary so it doesn't burn.

2. Add the Cajun seasoning and allow the spices to bloom in the fat for a few seconds, then stir in the butter. When the butter has melted, pour into a small bowl and set aside.

-recipe & ingredients continue-

SHELLFISH BOIL

1 tablespoon **extra-virgin olive oil**

2 **celery stalks,** diced

1 medium **yellow onion,** diced

1 **green bell pepper,** diced

Salt and **freshly ground black pepper**

1 cup **Pomi brand strained tomatoes**

1¼ cups **light beer**

2 pounds **mussels,** debearded and soaked in cool water

2 pounds **shrimp,** peeled and deveined

2 tablespoons chopped **fresh parsley**

2 **lemons,** cut into wedges

MAKE THE SHELLFISH BOIL

3. Return the pot to the stove and add the olive oil, along with the celery, onion, and bell pepper and sauté for 2 minutes. Season with salt and black pepper and sauté for 1 minute more.

4. Add the strained tomatoes and simmer for 3 minutes. Pour in the beer and bring to a simmer. Drain the mussels and add to the pot, along with the shrimp. Cover and cook for 5 minutes, stirring halfway through.

5. Discard any mussels that don't open, then distribute the open mussels and shrimp with the vegetables and liquid among eight bowls. Pour the Cajun garlic butter over the top of each bowl. Garnish with the parsley and serve with the lemon wedges alongside.

Roasted Beets
with Salad Agrodolce

AGRODOLCE, which means "sour and sweet" in Italian, is a sticky, tart, spicy condiment originating in Sicily. Usually served over grilled meats or as an accompaniment to cheese, the concentrated honey-and-vinegar glaze is the perfect match to earthy, tender roasted beets and freshly shaved ricotta salata. I love this salad as a starter for simply delicious meat dishes, like Perfect Pan-Basted Steak au Jus (page 205) or Pork Chops in Citrus Mojo Chino Latino (page 235). Be warned when serving this salad as a first course: It'll steal the show.

ROASTED BEETS

6 medium or
8 small **beets**

Extra-virgin olive oil

½ cup **red wine vinegar**

Salt and **freshly
ground black pepper**

1. Preheat the oven to 350°F.

TO ROAST THE BEETS

2. Clean the beets and trim off the roots and tops.

3. Cut a 12-inch square of foil and layer with parchment paper on top. Place 3 medium or 4 small beets on the parchment paper. Drizzle with enough olive oil to coat the beets in a thin layer of oil. Pour ¼ cup of the red wine vinegar over the beets and season with salt and pepper. Fold and crimp the parchment paper and foil to seal, forming a packet. Repeat with the remaining beets, olive oil, vinegar, and salt and pepper to make a second packet.

4. Place the beet packets on a sheet pan and roast until the beets are fork-tender, 1 to 1½ hours.

5. Allow the beets to cool, wrapped in foil, for 30 minutes to 1 hour. Once cool, peel by pinching off the skins, using a paring knife for hard-to-peel sections. Cut into bite-size pieces and set aside.

AGRODOLCE

3 cups **balsamic vinegar**

½ cup **red wine vinegar**

⅔ cup **honey**

2 tablespoons **extra-virgin olive oil**

1 small **red onion,** thinly sliced

¼ teaspoon **red chile flakes**

3 cups **raisins**

¼ cup chopped **roasted almonds**

SALAD

16 ounces **arugula**

6 ounces **ricotta salata**

MEANWHILE, MAKE THE AGRODOLCE

6. In a medium bowl, combine the balsamic vinegar, red wine vinegar, and honey.

7. In a sauté pan, heat the olive oil over medium-high heat. Add the red onion and sauté until lightly browned, about 5 minutes. Add the chile flakes and cook for about 30 seconds. Add the balsamic mixture, raisins, and almonds and simmer until slightly reduced, 2 to 3 minutes. Set aside to cool for 5 minutes.

TO ASSEMBLE THE SALADS

8. Divide the arugula among eight serving plates. Distribute the roasted beets among the plates, then dress with the agrodolce. Use a vegetable peeler to shave the ricotta salata over the salads.

Classic Lasagna Bolognese

CREDITED as one of the first pasta dishes ever created, lasagna's name comes from the Ancient Roman word *lasanum,* meaning "cooking pot." The first written record of lasagna dates to a thirteenth-century poem written by a Bolognese notary, and later recorded recipes called for dough that was fermented, flattened, sprinkled with cheese and spices, and then eaten with a pointed stick (maybe it was an early version of a toothpick?). Hundreds of years later, you can see how far we've come with my no-fuss, contemporary take on lasagna Bolognese, where beef takes the place of the more traditional veal. No need for pointed sticks, fermenting, flattening, or even precooking the lasagna sheets: No-boil noodles are an excellent way to get the lasagna into the oven faster.

Growing up, lasagna of any kind was a privilege. And lasagna Bolognese? Unheard of! If my mom ever had her hands on nice meat, she couldn't bear to hide it in layers of baked pasta. To this day, lasagna Bolognese still feels like a luxury—maybe even borderline rebellious—and perfect for a special occasion. This is my favorite recipe for when I really want to go all-out and be totally indulgent.

4 tablespoons **unsalted butter**

¼ cup **all-purpose flour**

3 cups **whole milk,** lukewarm

2½ cups grated **Parmesan cheese**

4 tablespoons **extra-virgin olive oil**

6 **garlic cloves,** minced

1. Preheat the oven to 375°F.

2. In a saucepan, melt the butter over medium heat. Stir in the flour and cook for 1 minute. Gradually whisk in the milk and cook until thickened, about 8 minutes. Whisk in the Parmesan and set the sauce aside.

3. In a separate saucepan, heat 2 tablespoons of the olive oil. Add the garlic and cook until browned, about 3 minutes. Stir in the chile flakes and basil. Pour in the tomato puree, season with a pinch of salt, and cook for 15 minutes.

-recipe & ingredients continue-

Pinch of
red chile flakes

25 **basil leaves,** torn

1 (24.5-ounce) bottle
tomato puree (passata)

Salt and **freshly
ground black pepper**

1 pound **ground beef**

1 pound **Delverde
instant lasagna sheets,**
soaked in water

1 pound **whole-milk
mozzarella cheese,**
grated

4. Meanwhile, in a sauté pan, heat the remaining 2 tablespoons olive oil over high heat. Add the beef and a pinch of salt and cook, using a wooden spoon to break up the meat, until browned, about 5 minutes.

5. Pour the tomato sauce over the beef and simmer for 5 minutes. Taste and adjust the seasoning with salt and black pepper.

6. Spoon ½ cup of the Bolognese sauce over the bottom of an 8-inch square baking dish. Top with a layer of lasagna sheets. Cover with more sauce, then repeat until all the pasta sheets have been used.

7. Pour the cheese sauce over the top, sprinkle with the mozzarella, and cover with foil.

8. Bake according to the directions on the lasagna sheet package or until the cheese is golden brown, removing the foil in the final few minutes.

Slow Pasta Genovese alla Rafi

LA GENOVESE is a meat sauce that's cooked low and slow in aromatic broth until the meat tenderizes to the point that it's falling apart. Most likely brought to Naples by immigrants from Genoa (Genovese means "in the style of Genoa"), this hearty dish has since become synonymous with southern Italian cuisine. This recipe was inspired by a restaurant in Sorrento, where Chef Rafi waxed poetic on the beauty of a slow-simmered meal. Economical, easy to make, and satisfying, this one is worth a few extra minutes on the stove. Make a big batch and enjoy it all week long.

3½ pounds **beef stew meat**

Salt and **freshly ground black pepper**

1 pound **pancetta**, diced

4 **celery stalks**, diced

1 large **carrot**, diced

4 pounds **yellow onions**, diced

¼ cup **tomato paste**

1 pound **paccheri pasta**

1. Season the beef with salt and pepper.

2. Place a large Dutch oven over medium-high heat. Add the pancetta and cook until translucent, 4 to 5 minutes. In batches, add the stew meat and sear on all sides in the pancetta fat. Remove the stew meat (leaving the pancetta in the pan) and set aside.

3. Add the celery, carrot, and onions to the Dutch oven and cook until tender, about 5 minutes. Add the tomato paste and cook, stirring, for 1 minute.

4. Return the stew meat to the pot and add water to cover by about 2 inches. Bring to a boil. Reduce the heat to maintain a simmer, cover, and cook until the meat is tender and falling apart, about 45 minutes.

5. When the beef is almost ready, bring a large pot of generously salted water to a boil. Add the pasta to the boiling water and cook to al dente according to the package directions. Drain.

6. Spoon the Genovese sauce over a bed of cooked paccheri and serve.

Made-for-the-Kids Hot Chili BBQ Ribs

WHEN IT COMES to pork, I consider ribs to be the king of all cuts. These hot chili BBQ ribs are my favorite, with their fall-off-the-bone-tender meat and sticky, sweet, and spicy glaze. Because rib rack is surrounded by a layer of fat, cooking on the bone not only adds richness to the meat, it also keeps it from drying out. Pork ribs, with all their meat being in direct contact with the bone, take a while to cook but are well worth the time and added effort. Here the ribs are first oven-braised in foil, then glazed with a Korean gochujang sauce which is just spicy enough for the adults but sweet enough for the kids. It's then finished on the grill until smoky and caramelized. Though you'll need to be near your kitchen for a few hours, these ribs require little active work. A few store-bought condiments and simple techniques produce an unbelievably flavorful, juicy, and delicious dish that's fun to share.

RIBS

1 heaping cup **light brown sugar**

¾ cup **apple cider vinegar**

6 tablespoons **ketchup**

3 tablespoons **chili crisp**

2 tablespoons **liquid smoke**

8 **garlic cloves,** sliced

2 (10- to 13-rib) racks **baby back ribs**

Salt and **freshly ground black pepper**

Paprika

1. Preheat the oven to 425°F.

TO PREPARE THE RIBS

2. In a bowl, combine the brown sugar, vinegar, ketchup, chili crisp, liquid smoke, and garlic.

3. Split the racks in half and season generously with salt, pepper, and paprika.

4. Cut a 2-foot section of foil and place parchment paper on top. Rub one-quarter of the brown sugar mixture on one of the rack sections and place on the parchment paper. Fold the edges of the parchment and foil to seal, creating a bag. Repeat with the remaining ribs and brown sugar mixture.

5. Place the wrapped ribs on a sheet pan and roast for 30 minutes.

6. Reduce the oven temperature to 275°F and continue cooking for 1 hour.

RIB SAUCE

1¼ cups **ketchup**

½ cup **apple cider vinegar**

5 tablespoons **honey**

¼ cup **gochujang** (Korean chile paste)

2 tablespoons **toasted sesame oil**

Coleslaw or **baked sweet potatoes,** for serving

7. Remove the ribs from the oven and allow to rest, wrapped in the foil, for 30 minutes.

MEANWHILE, MAKE THE RIB SAUCE

8. In a medium bowl, combine the ketchup, vinegar, honey, gochujang, and sesame oil.

9. Fire up the grill to high.

10. Brush the rib sauce on the ribs and kiss them on the grill until the sauce caramelizes on each side, 1 to 2 minutes per side.

11. Divide among four serving plates and serve with a simple coleslaw or baked sweet potatoes on the side.

Lobster *with Lemony Red Pepper Butter & Popovers*

THERE ARE few things quite as festive as puffed popovers hot out of the oven, steamed lobster, and melted butter. Here I serve the crustaceans with simple savory popovers—named for the batter's ability to rise and "pop over" the tin while baking—and a bright and spicy butter sauce.

The best thing about this dish, besides its full flavor and wow-worthy presentation, is that the lobster and butter come together quickly and easily, and the popovers can be made up to 2 hours in advance. Simply prick them with a fork to keep them from deflating, cool on a wire rack, and reheat for 5 to 6 minutes in a 250°F oven before serving.

POPOVERS

4 cups **all-purpose flour**

5 teaspoons **salt**

4 cups **whole milk**

8 large **eggs**

Cooking spray

10 ounces shredded **cheddar cheese**

TO MAKE THE POPOVERS

1. Place two 6-cup popover pans or one 12-cup muffin tin in the oven and preheat the oven to 350°F.

2. Place the flour and salt in a fine-mesh sieve and sift onto a piece of wax paper.

3. In a small saucepan, heat the milk over medium heat until small bubbles appear around the edges of the pan.

4. In a large bowl, whisk the eggs until frothy. Gradually whisk the hot milk into the eggs, being careful to add the milk slowly so as not to cook the eggs.

5. Cone the wax paper to pick up the flour mixture. Gradually whisk it into the egg mixture and stir until almost smooth (a few lumps are fine).

-recipe & ingredients continue-

LOBSTERS

8 (1½-pound) **lobsters**

**LEMONY RED
PEPPER BUTTER**

2 (9-ounce) jars
**Tracklements
Fresh Chilli Jam**

Grated zest and
juice of 4 **lemons**

2 sticks (8 ounces)
unsalted butter

Salt and **freshly
ground black pepper**

6. Remove the hot popover pans from the oven and mist the cups with cooking spray. While the pans are still hot, fill each cup at least three-quarters of the way full with the batter. Divide the grated cheddar among the cups and place the pans on a baking sheet to catch any drips.

7. Bake the popovers for 15 minutes.

8. Rotate the pans front to back to ensure an even rise and bake until the popovers are golden brown, 35 minutes more.

MEANWHILE, PREPARE THE LOBSTERS

9. Place 2 cups water into each of two large pots and bring to a boil over high heat. (If you don't have two large pots, you can cook the lobsters in two batches.) Add 4 lobsters to each pot, cover, and steam until just cooked through, 8 to 10 minutes.

MEANWHILE, MAKE THE LEMONY RED PEPPER BUTTER

10. In a saucepan, heat the jam, lemon zest, and lemon juice over medium heat until simmering. Whisk in the butter and bring back to a simmer. Remove from the heat and season with salt and pepper to taste.

11. Plate the whole lobsters with cracking utensils and the lemony red pepper butter on the side.

12. Invert the pans to remove the popovers and serve alongside the lobsters.

Fried Rice Balls
with Mozzarella (aka Supplì)

I LOVE GREETING my guests at home with this Roman street food as soon as they walk through the door. Think of supplì as a smaller cousin of Sicilian arancini, another cheesy finger food I've seen popping up on trendy bar menus in recent years. Here, risotto is stuffed with mozzarella, formed into an egg-shaped ball, coated in bread crumbs, and fried until melty and delicious. It's perfect for indulgent snacking or entertaining.

RISOTTO

3 cups **chicken stock**

Extra-virgin olive oil

½ small **yellow onion,** finely diced

¾ cup **Arborio rice**

¾ cup bottled **tomato puree** (passata)

Salt and **freshly ground black pepper**

4 tablespoons **unsalted butter**

¾ cup grated **Parmesan cheese**

TO MAKE THE RISOTTO

1. In a small saucepan, heat the chicken stock over medium heat until it begins to steam. Set aside and keep warm.

2. In a deep saucepan, heat enough olive oil to cover the bottom of the pan over medium-high heat. Add the onion and sauté until translucent, about 7 minutes. Add the rice and toast, stirring continuously, for 2 to 3 minutes. This gives the risotto more texture.

3. Add 1 cup of the chicken stock and ¼ cup of the tomato puree. Cook, stirring regularly to evenly incorporate the liquid, until the pan is almost dry. Once almost all the liquid has been absorbed into the rice, continue adding the stock and tomato puree in increments until all the stock and puree have been added and the risotto is perfectly al dente, about 12 minutes.

4. Season to taste with salt and pepper. Add the butter one tablespoon at a time and then the Parmesan and stir to combine.

5. Line a baking sheet with parchment paper and spread the risotto in an even layer over the paper. Transfer to the refrigerator to cool for about 1 hour.

-recipe & ingredients continue-

SUPPLÌ

2 large **eggs**, beaten

1 cup **Italian seasoned bread crumbs**

Salt

3 ounces **mozzarella cheese,** diced

Neutral oil, for frying

Marinara sauce, for serving

MAKE THE SUPPLÌ

6. Set up a dredging station with two shallow dishes: Place the egg in one bowl. Place the bread crumbs in the other and season them with salt to taste.

7. Cut the cooled risotto into 1½-inches long by 1-inch wide. Taking one of the rectangles in your hand, add some of the diced mozzarella cheese to the center. Lay another risotto rectangle on top and use your hands to seal the sides and form the risotto into a small egg shape, completely enclosing the cheese. Repeat until all the risotto and mozzarella are used.

8. Once all the supplì are formed, dip them in the egg and toss in the bread crumbs to coat.

9. Pour 2 inches of neutral oil into a deep pot or Dutch oven and heat over medium heat to 325°F.

10. Working in batches, fry the supplì until they're golden brown, about 5 minutes.

11. Serve hot with marinara sauce.

Devils on Horseback Salad

I MAKE THIS traditional British appetizer for every holiday because it's sweet, funky, salty, and delicious, but also because it's easy. With sweet dates, blue cheese, bacon, walnuts, and ripe pears, these hit all the flavors you want in a holiday dish. The stuffed dates are meant to be served "devilishly" hot, but make sure to resist the smell of melty blue cheese, gooey dates, and salty bacon filling your kitchen for a few minutes to give the caramelized sugar time to cool before digging in.

DEVILS ON HORSEBACK

12 ounces **Medjool dates** (about 40)

8 ounces **blue cheese**

2 **pears**, cored and thinly sliced

1½ pounds **applewood-smoked bacon**

LITTLE GEM SALAD

1 cup **walnuts**

2 tablespoons **Dijon mustard**

¼ cup **sherry vinegar**

½ cup **extra-virgin olive oil**

Salt and **freshly ground black pepper**

1 pound **Little Gem lettuces**, cored

TO MAKE THE DEVILS ON HORSEBACK

1. Preheat the broiler to high.

2. Using a paring knife, cut a lengthwise slit down the middle of each date and pull out the pit. Press a small amount of blue cheese inside the cavity of each date and slide one slice of pear inside.

3. Cut the bacon slices into 2-inch lengths and wrap each date with a piece of bacon.

4. Lay the stuffed dates seam-side down in a single layer in a broilerproof baking dish and broil until the bacon is cooked and the cheese is soft, about 3 to 5 minutes. Set aside to cool slightly.

MEANWHILE, MAKE THE LITTLE GEM SALAD

5. In a small dry sauté pan, toast the walnuts over medium heat for 3 to 5 minutes. Tip onto a plate and set aside.

6. In a large bowl, whisk together the mustard and vinegar. Keep whisking as you gradually pour in the olive oil. Season with salt and pepper.

7. Toss the Little Gem lettuce in the dressing and arrange on eight plates. Top each salad with the cooled stuffed dates and the toasted walnuts.

My Ultimate Fried Chicken

WHILE FRYING CHICKEN may seem intimidating, it's actually a surefire way to get tender, juicy chicken with a crispy golden brown crust, every time. In fact, it's hard to overcook fried chicken—especially this one, which is first brined to tenderize and flavor the meat, then dipped in tangy buttermilk, double-breaded, and fried to crispy-on-the-outside, moist-on-the-inside perfection.

I like buying whole chicken because it tends to be higher quality and less expensive. Plus, you get to experience all the different cuts of the bird. That said, if you don't feel like butchering the chicken yourself, you can ask your butcher to cut up the chicken for you. If you *do* feel like butchering the chicken yourself and haven't done so before, I commend your curiosity! It's a useful and fun skill to keep in your arsenal. Check out the hundreds of videos on the internet for help—and make sure to use a very sharp knife.

BRINED CHICKEN

1 (3- to 5-pound) **whole chicken,** cut into 8 serving pieces

2 tablespoons **salt**

1 tablespoon **ground white pepper**

2 teaspoons **chili powder**

2 teaspoons **garlic powder**

2 teaspoons **onion powder**

1 teaspoon **cayenne pepper**

TO BRINE THE CHICKEN

1. Place the chicken pieces in a large container. Sprinkle them with the salt, white pepper, chili powder, garlic powder, onion powder, and cayenne. Pour in enough water to submerge the chicken. Refrigerate for 4 hours to brine. Drain and set aside.

TO FRY THE CHICKEN

2. Pour 2½ quarts of neutral oil into a large dutch oven and heat over medium heat to 300°F. Preheat the oven to 325°F. Line a sheet tray with a wire rack and set aside.

FOR FRYING

Neutral oil

2 cups
all-purpose flour

1 tablespoon
garlic powder

1 tablespoon
onion powder

1 teaspoon **cayenne
pepper**

Ground white pepper

Salt

1 cup **buttermilk**

2 large **egg
whites,** beaten

3. Meanwhile, set up a dredging station in two large bowls: In one bowl, stir together the flour, garlic powder, onion powder, cayenne, 1 tablespoon white pepper, and salt to taste and mix to combine. In the second bowl, whisk together the buttermilk, egg whites, and salt and white pepper to taste.

4. Add the drained chicken pieces to the flour mixture, one piece at a time, tossing to coat all around. Shake off any excess flour from the chicken. Add to the buttermilk mixture to coat. Pull the chicken out of the buttermilk and dredge again in the flour mix.

5. Working in batches, add the chicken to the hot oil and fry until golden and crispy, about 14 to 16 minutes depending on the cut. Transfer to the prepared sheet tray.

6. When all the chicken is done, slide the pan in the oven and bake until the internal temperature reaches 165°F, about 10 minutes.

Serves 4

Total Time: **40 minutes**

Ease of Preparation: **Easy**

Spring Saffron Risotto
with Chicken

WHILE RISOTTO is often pointed to as a test of a chef's ability to achieve the elusive "rice suspended in sauce" consistency, preparing risotto at home is quite easy. This vibrant yellow risotto is tinted and flavored by saffron, an almost otherworldly spice with floral, sweet, and earthy notes that must be experienced to be understood. The rest is simple, with just a few basic rules of thumb to never skip when it comes to making risotto. First, you need high-quality chicken stock—homemade or store-bought organic bone broth works well—and it needs to be warm when you add it to ensure the grains of rice cook evenly. And second, yes, you really do need to stir the entire time. Stirring releases the rice's starch to create a creamy, velvety consistency.

I love this risotto in the spring when fresh peas are thriving and I have to stop myself from putting them in every dish I make. Seared chicken breasts add heartiness, but this risotto can be served with just about any protein, or even stand on its own.

3 tablespoons
extra-virgin olive oil

2 **boneless, skinless
chicken breasts**, cut
into large chunks

Salt and **freshly
ground black pepper**

½ cup shelled **fresh peas**

2 quarts
chicken stock

2 teaspoons
saffron threads

1. In a sauté pan, heat 1 tablespoon of the olive oil over medium heat. Season the chicken with salt and pepper. Add to the pan and sear until golden brown and three-quarters of the way cooked, about 10 minutes.

2. In a medium bowl, make an ice bath by combining equal parts water and ice. Bring a small pot of salted water to a boil. Add the peas and cook for 1 minute, then drain and add to the ice bath.

3. In a medium saucepan, warm the chicken stock. Add the saffron, cover, and bring to a simmer over high heat. Once simmering, turn off the heat and leave the pan covered.

-recipe & ingredients continue-

1 stick (4 ounces)
grass-fed butter

1 medium **yellow onion,**
finely diced

2 cups **Arborio** or
Carnaroli rice

1 cup **dry white wine**

1 cup grated
Parmesan cheese

4. Meanwhile, in a large saucepan, melt 4 tablespoons of the butter in the remaining 2 tablespoons olive oil over medium-high heat. Add the onion and cook until slightly softened, about 3 minutes. Add the rice and stir until all the rice is hot and toasted, about 4 minutes. Season with salt and pepper.

5. Add the white wine and stir until the wine has evaporated. Add a ladleful of the chicken stock, bring to a simmer, and cook, stirring, until all the liquid has been absorbed.

6. Continue to add the remaining chicken stock in small batches, cooking and stirring over low to medium heat until the rice has absorbed most of the broth and you have a very loose-looking porridge. The rice should be cooked but still toothsome.

7. Drain the peas and stir them into the rice with the remaining 4 tablespoons butter and half the Parmesan.

8. Taste and adjust the seasoning, then add the cooked chicken to the rice and stir.

9. Spoon the rice evenly into four bowls and top with the remaining Parmesan.

Fried Chicken Meatballs
in Spicy Vodka Sauce

WITH "MOST SEARCHED" being a modern-day popularity contest, vodka sauce holds the title for the most popular classic pasta sauce to make at home. It's well-known for its rich, velvety texture and ability to come together quickly with just a few simple ingredients. Here a simple vodka pasta gets an upgrade with herby pan-seared meatballs.

To make the spicy vodka sauce, I use passata, an uncooked tomato puree that yields a fresh tomato flavor that plays well with the savory meatballs. It's spiced with 1 teaspoon of red chile flakes, which is plenty of kick for most, but feel free to add more if you're feeling brave. The creamy, spicy sauce and crispy meatballs are an easy match—you'll want plenty of bread to soak it all up.

CHICKEN MEATBALLS

1 slice **white bread,** torn

¼ cup **whole milk**

1 tablespoon plus ¼ cup **extra-virgin olive oil**

1 **garlic clove,** minced

¼ cup minced **yellow onion**

½ teaspoon **red chile flakes**

Salt and **freshly ground black pepper**

1 pound **ground chicken**

1 large **egg,** beaten

TO MAKE THE CHICKEN MEATBALLS

1. Place the bread in a small bowl and pour in the milk. Press the milk into the bread.

2. In a small pan, heat the tablespoon of olive oil over medium heat. Add the garlic and cook until browned, about 3 minutes. Stir in the onion, chile flakes, and a pinch of salt and cook until the onion is translucent, about 8 minutes. Remove from the heat and set aside to cool.

3. In a large bowl, combine the cooled onion and garlic mixture, the soaked bread, ground chicken, egg, parsley, and basil. Season with salt and black pepper to taste and stir to combine. Divide the mixture into 12 portions and shape into meatballs.

4. In a sauté pan, heat the remaining ¼ cup of olive oil over medium heat. Add the meatballs and brown them on all sides, using a spoon to roll them around the pan. Remove the meatballs and set aside.

1 tablespoon chopped **fresh parsley,** plus more for garnish

1 tablespoon chopped **fresh basil,** plus more for garnish

SPICY VODKA SAUCE

2 teaspoons minced **garlic**

3 tablespoons minced **yellow onion**

1 teaspoon **red chile flakes**

¼ cup **vodka**

1½ cups bottled **tomato puree** (passata)

⅓ cup **heavy cream**

½ cup freshly grated **Parmesan cheese**

Salt and **freshly ground black pepper**

Handful of chopped parsley and basil

Cooked pasta or **crusty bread,** for serving

5. Add the garlic to the oil in the sauté pan and sauté over medium heat until lightly browned, about 2 minutes. Add the onion and sauté for 2 minutes. Add the chile flakes and stir to combine. Pour in the vodka and allow the alcohol to evaporate for 1 minute.

6. Pour in the tomato puree and bring everything to a simmer. Once simmering, return the meatballs to the pan and cook in the sauce for 10 minutes.

7. Stir in the cream. Allow the sauce to come back to a simmer, then stir in the Parmesan. Taste and adjust the seasoning with salt and black pepper.

8. Garnish with chopped parsley and basil and serve over cooked pasta or with toasted crusty bread on the side.

Spiced Herb Butter Spatchcocked Turkey
with All the Fixings

IF MAKING AN entire Thanksgiving dinner with all the fixings in under two hours isn't enough of a case for spatchcocking your turkey, this recipe is sure to convince you. The turkey's crispy skin and tender meat gets evenly cooked throughout—unlike every whole turkey ever, no matter how skilled the chef. Here I lay out my full process for Thanksgiving dinner step by step, from start to finish. My favorite sides, the true star of any Thanksgiving table, are all invited, gathered from years of testing, refining, and narrowing down the most nostalgic and deeply delicious recipes I've collected throughout my life.

SPATCHCOCKED TURKEY

1 (13- to 15-pound) **whole turkey**

1. Gather and prepare all the ingredients before you begin cooking, including for any sides dishes you are making.

2. Place an oven rack in upper third of the oven and preheat the oven to 450°F.

TO SPATCHCOCK THE TURKEY

3. Remove any excess fat and leftover pinfeathers from the turkey and pat the outside dry. Using sharp kitchen shears or a cleaver, cut along both sides of the backbone and remove it from the turkey. Cut the backbone and the neck crosswise into 1-inch pieces. Set both aside for making the gravy.

4. Flatten the turkey by placing it skin-side up on a cutting board and applying firm pressure to the breastbone until it cracks and becomes noticeably flatter.

-recipe & ingredients continue-

GRAVY BROTH

1 **leek**

¼ cup **extra-virgin olive oil**

1 cup diced **carrots**

½ cup diced **celery**

1 teaspoon **black peppercorns**

3 **bay leaves**

1 **thyme sprig**

10 cups **water**

BRAISING VEGETABLES

1 cup diced **celery**

2 cups diced **carrots**

4 **shallots**, quartered

1 head **garlic**, halved horizontally

2 (14.5-ounce) cans **chicken stock**

SPICED HERB BUTTER

2 sticks (8 ounces) **unsalted butter**

5 teaspoons **salt**

1 teaspoon **freshly ground black pepper**

2 tablespoons chopped **fresh herbs,** such as thyme, tarragon, rosemary, and oregano

3 tablespoons chopped **fresh parsley**

TO MAKE THE GRAVY BROTH

5. Slice the green top off the leek and wash it thoroughly to remove any grit in between the leaves. Cut into 1-inch pieces. Set the white part of the leek aside for the braising vegetables (see step 9).

6. In a large saucepan, heat the olive oil over high heat until shimmering. Add the turkey backbone and neck pieces. Stir frequently until well browned, about 3 minutes.

7. Add the leek greens, carrots, celery, peppercorns, bay leaves, and thyme. Cook, stirring frequently, until the vegetables begin to brown, about 3 minutes.

8. Add the water and use a wooden spoon to scrape up any browned bits from the bottom of the pan. Reduce the heat to maintain a simmer and cook for 40 minutes while the turkey and vegetables roast.

TO PREPARE THE BRAISING VEGETABLES

9. Working with the white part of the leek (reserved from step 5), discard the outer layers and slice crosswise into ¼-inch-thick rounds. Place in a bowl of water so any soil that's stuck between the layers sinks to the bottom. Rinse well and drain.

10. In a roasting pan, combine the leek whites, celery, carrots, shallots, halved garlic head, and chicken stock.

11. Position the turkey over the vegetables so the breasts are aligned with the center of the roasting pan and the legs are close to the edge.

TO MAKE THE SPICED HERB BUTTER

12. In a saucepan, melt the butter over medium heat. Add the salt, pepper, chopped herbs, and parsley and stir to combine.

13. Brush the spiced herb butter inside the skin and all over the turkey, including in the cavity. Roast the turkey for 30 minutes.

-recipe & ingredients continue-

THE FIXINGS

Cranberry Sauce
(recipe follows)

Candied Bacon Brussels Sprouts (recipe follows)

Candied Butternut Squash Whipped Mash (recipe follows)

Lemon-Zested Chestnut and Sourdough Stuffing (recipe follows)

GRAVY

Gravy Broth
(see page 284)

¼ cup **water**

¼ cup **cornstarch**

Salt and **freshly ground black pepper**

TO PREPARE TO COOK THE FIXINGS

14. Once the turkey goes into the oven, prepare the cranberry sauce, candied Brussels sprouts, butternut squash mash, and sourdough stuffing. Stick the Brussels sprouts, squash, and stuffing into the oven once the temperature has been reduced to 375°F, staging them as needed depending on oven rack space. Note that you will have time to finish any of these dishes while the turkey is resting.

15. Remove the turkey from the oven and reduce the oven temperature to 375°F. Baste the turkey with its own pan juices. If the turkey is starting to look dry, cover it with foil. Return the turkey to the oven and roast until it's cooked through, 45 minutes to 1 hour. To check, insert an instant-read thermometer at the thickest part of the breast, close to bone (but not touching it): It should register 150°F. The joint between the thighs and body should register at least 155°F.

16. Remove the turkey from the oven, transfer to a cutting board, tent loosely with foil, and allow to rest for at least 30 minutes before carving.

TO MAKE THE GRAVY

17. Strain the turkey pan juices into a medium pot. Strain the aromatic gravy broth into the pot with the pan juices and stir to combine. Boil over medium-high heat for about 7 minutes, until reduced, then remove from the heat and set aside until ready to finish the gravy (just before serving).

18. Just before serving, in a small bowl, combine the water and cornstarch to make a slurry. Pour the slurry into the gravy, boil for another 5 minutes, then taste and adjust the seasoning with salt and pepper.

19. To serve, garnish the turkey with any extra herbs you may have. Present at the table, then carve and serve with the hot gravy and all the fixings.

-recipe & ingredients continue-

Cranberry Sauce

Makes 2 cups

1 cup **fresh cranberries**

¾ cup **water**

¼ cup **sugar**

¼ teaspoon grated **orange zest**

Juice of 1 **orange**

¼ teaspoon **ground cinnamon**

1 teaspoon **citrus pectin**

1. Add the cranberries to a large zip-seal bag. Seal the bag and pop the berries by hitting them with the flat side of a meat mallet or the bottom of a small pot.

2. Transfer the cranberries to a microwave-safe bowl. Stir in the water, sugar, orange zest, orange juice, and cinnamon. Microwave on high for 3 minutes.

3. Remove the bowl and carefully sprinkle in the pectin while whisking to dissolve, making sure there are no clumps. Microwave again for 1½ minutes. Set aside.

Candied Bacon Brussels Sprouts

Serves 8

2 pounds **Brussels sprouts**, trimmed, halved, and rinsed

Extra-virgin olive oil

Salt and **freshly ground black pepper**

8 ounces **smoked bacon**, cut crosswise into strips ½ inch wide

Leaves from 1 **rosemary sprig**

¼ cup **honey**

1. Preheat the oven to 375°F.

2. Place the Brussels sprouts on a sheet pan and drizzle with some olive oil. Season with salt and pepper.

3. Transfer to the oven and roast until tender and browned, 10 to 15 minutes.

4. Meanwhile, in a sauté pan, cook the bacon over medium heat until it starts to brown, about 5 minutes. Add the rosemary leaves and honey and let caramelize for about 6 minutes.

5. Add the roasted Brussels sprouts to the pan and toss to combine.

Candied Butternut Squash Whipped Mash

2 large **butternut squash,** halved lengthwise and seeded

Extra-virgin olive oil

Salt and **freshly ground black pepper**

4 **thyme sprigs**

4 **garlic cloves,** peeled and whole

1 stick (4 ounces) **unsalted butter**

3 tablespoons **honey**

½ teaspoon **ground cinnamon**

⅛ teaspoon **ground allspice**

½ cup **crème fraîche**

1 cup **mini marshmallows**

1 cup **hazelnuts,** crushed

¼ cup packed **light brown sugar**

2 tablespoons **water**

1. Preheat the oven to 375°F. Line a sheet pan with parchment paper.

2. Place the butternut squash halves cut-side up on the lined pan. Drizzle the cavities with some olive oil and season generously with salt and pepper. Flip the squash over so they're cut-side down. Slide a sprig of thyme and 1 garlic clove inside each cavity for aroma.

3. Transfer the butternut squash to the oven and roast until fork-tender, about 45 minutes. Leave the oven on.

4. When cool enough to handle, discard thyme and garlic clovers and scoop the squash flesh into a bowl. Add 4 tablespoons of the butter, the honey, cinnamon, allspice, and crème fraîche. Mash and adjust the seasoning with more salt and pepper.

5. Spread the mash in a 6 x 8-inch baking dish and sprinkle the marshmallows and hazelnuts on top.

6. In a small saucepan, melt the remaining 4 tablespoons butter. Add the brown sugar and let the sugar dissolve. Pour in the water and let the mixture bubble up.

7. Pour the mixture over the butternut squash, transfer to the oven, and bake until the sugar begins to caramelize and brown, about 10 minutes.

-recipe & ingredients continue-

Lemon-Zested Chestnut & Sourdough Stuffing

Serves 8

12 ounces **sour-dough bread**, diced

4 tablespoons **unsalted butter**

5 ounces peeled **chestnuts**, chopped

Leaves from 1 **rosemary sprig**

½ cup finely diced **celery**

2 cups finely diced **yellow onions**

1 cup finely diced **carrots**

1 cup **chicken stock**, plus more as necessary

Salt and **freshly ground black pepper**

Grated zest of 1 **lemon**

1. Preheat the oven to 375°F.

2. Place the sourdough on a sheet pan and toast in the oven for 10 minutes.

3. In a large sauté pan, melt the butter over medium heat. Add the chestnuts and rosemary and cook for 1 minute. Add the celery, onions, and carrots and cook, stirring, until the vegetables are tender, about 3 minutes.

4. Stir in the toasted sourdough and pour in the chicken stock. If the mixture looks dry, add a touch more stock. Season with salt, pepper, and the lemon zest.

Candied Bacon Burger Bloody Mary

IF I'M going to drink a Bloody Mary, I want it to feel like a full meal. In fact, I measure the quality of a restaurant's Bloody Mary based on its garnishes: It should look like the cocktail version of going all-out on a giant spread or seafood tower at your favorite breakfast spot. That's the all-day Sunday brunch spirit I'm going for here, with what's probably an excessive number of toppings, most of which can be purchased at the market or are quick and easy to make, like a shrimp cocktail made of store-bought cooked shrimp.

Mini cheeseburger sliders propped up on long skewers are charming and hilarious, and I recommend them if you have the time. Though I love every one of these garnishes, one Bloody Mary can only hold so much. Pick and choose the ones that most appeal to you.

BLOODY MARYS

Celery salt

Ice

1 ounce **fresh lemon juice**

1 ounce **fresh lime juice**

8 ounces **vodka**

16 ounces **tomato juice**

¼ ounce **Tabasco sauce**

¼ ounce **Worcestershire sauce**

2½ tablespoons **prepared horseradish**

2 teaspoons **freshly ground black pepper**

2 teaspoons **smoked paprika**

1. Rim four highball glasses or one giant glass with celery salt. Add ice to the glass(es).

2. In an extra-large ice-filled cocktail shaker, combine the lemon juice, lime juice, vodka, tomato juice, Tabasco, Worcestershire, horseradish, pepper, smoked paprika, and 2 teaspoons celery salt. Shake until completely chilled and strain into the glass(es).

**GARNISHES
(PICK YOUR FAVORITES)**

Parsley sprigs

Green olives

Lime wedges

Lemon wedges

Celery stalks

Cheeseburger sliders

Candied bacon
(see Note)

Cornichons

Cocktail onions

Cooked shrimp

3. Skewer the garnishes, loading on as many as will fit. Place the skewer(s) in the glass(es) and enjoy.

Note: To make candied bacon, preheat the oven to 350°F. Lay slices of bacon on a sheet pan and sprinkle with brown sugar or drizzle with maple syrup. Bake until crispy, about 15 minutes. Transfer to a wire rack to cool.

Index

About the Author

Rocco DiSpirito is a James Beard Award-winning chef and author of fourteen books, including three #1 *New York Times* bestsellers. Rocco began his culinary studies at the Culinary Institute of America and by twenty was working in the kitchens of legendary chefs around the globe. He was named *Food & Wine* magazine's Best New Chef and was the first to appear on *Gourmet* magazine's cover as America's Most Exciting Young Chef. His three-star restaurant Union Pacific—where Ruth Reichl, in her famous *New York Times* review, said she "moaned as she ate"—was a culinary landmark for many years. Rocco has starred on numerous television shows. Most recently, he received two stars from the *New York Times* as chef of the critically acclaimed Standard Grill in New York City.

All rights reserved.
Published in the United States by
Rodale Books, an imprint of
Random House, a division of
Penguin Random House LLC, New York.
RodaleBooks.com
RandomHouseBooks.com

Rodale Books and the plant
colophon are registered trademarks
of Penguin Random House LLC.

Library of Congress Cataloging-in-
Publication Data has been applied for.

ISBN 978-1-9848-2523-0
Ebook ISBN 978-1-9848-2524-7

Printed in China

Book design by Jan Derevjanik
Cover photographs by Jonathan Pushnik

10 9 8 7 6 5 4 3 2 1

First Edition